DAYBREAK
WITHIN

DAYBREAK WITHIN

Living in a Sacred World

RICH HEFFERN

FOREST OF PEACE
Publishing

Suppliers for the Spiritual Pilgrim

DAYBREAK WITHIN

copyright © 1998, by Rich Heffern

Library of Congress Cataloging-in-Publication Data

Heffern, Rich.
    Daybreak within : living in a sacred world / Rich Heffern.
      p.   cm.
    ISBN 0-939516-41-1 (pbk.)
    1. Spirituality. 2. Spiritual life. 3. Lifestyles.
    4. Mysticism.   I. Title.
    BL624.H383 1998
    291.4'4—dc21   98-16331
                            CIP

published by

Forest of Peace Publishing, Inc.
PO Box 269
Leavenworth, KS 66048-0269   USA
1-800-659-3227

printed by

Hall Directory, Inc.
Topeka, KS 66608-0007

1st printing: April 1998

Dedication

to my wife
Linda

Yummy!

My deepest thanks and love to Bob and Sue in the Ozarks,
who live on and love the land there
in Mad Dog Hollow.

Thanks also to Art Winter, former editor of *Praying*,
the magazine of spirituality for everyday living,
for his encouragement and support.

Where can I go from your spirit?
From your presence where can I flee?

—Psalm 139

Contents

Introduction:

Aerial Reconnaissance of a Conflagration of the Heart

Not long ago I spent an evening talking with an old friend. Let's call him Paul. At first our conversation was news and pleasantries, but it soon took an abrupt turn. Paul was in a thoughtful mood. Christmas was approaching. We had just opened a bottle of good wine. As we talked, a news program flickered on the TV console that blocked his fireplace. The sound was off.

Paul is a salesman. He works smack in the middle of the electric hive of our city's commerce. He told tales of stress, of the breakneck pace. I got the picture quickly: weekdays choreographed to the rhythms of a Tilt-a-Whirl, weekends spent skittering out of breath through the shopping malls after oil filters, socks, cotton swabs, cassettes for the VCR. With equal parts love and dismay in his voice, he talked about his kids — how the neon pageantry, the beckonings and taunts of consumerism teased them, held them spellbound. No longer content with clover chains, kites or hopscotch, they were up to their dimpled elbows in battery-operated offerings from the toy industry. Paul was gearing up the budget for the annual winter rite of throwing cash and credit cards at the feet of the unappeasable gods of retail.

What he failed to say told me more about the state of his marriage than what he did relate. They had been married in a rose garden. Love had brought them together, and we had witnessed their pledging and celebrated it with eating, drinking and dancing. Together they had written the heartfelt words for the simple ceremony. Now the marriage seemed beleaguered, besieged by one damned thing after another; the magic pilfered out of it bit by bit. There was never enough time to renew the bonds, to sit back and simply cherish, to doodle in the margins of their passion and compassion for each other.

In Paul's eyes and at the corners of his mouth there was a sadness. He seemed to be making it — but all too joylessly. There was sunshine in his life, but too little warmth in it. He sounded disheartened and frazzled. There were no huge calamities in his life, true. Yet the circuitry of his spirit seemed corroded. He kicked one of his boy's plastic toys. A piece of it fell off.

Deep down, underlying all else, I sensed there was something lodged in his heart, a kind of outraged grief that smoldered there, darkening his world like a pall of windstrewn volcanic ash high aloft in the skies. Somehow the hurt and outrage seemed to arise from a sense of having been cheated out of his birthright as a man, as a human being. The birthright had been sold down the river for the price of a lifetime of empty novelties and barren entertainment.

An image of him came to mind as we talked. I saw him clad in a down vest astride a humpbacked granite boulder, with soaring, jagged ridges looming above him. In our younger days Paul and I had been backpacking buddies. Once long ago we took Amtrak to Wyoming, then hitchhiked up to the spectacularly rugged Wind River Mountains and spent a week scrambling across the Continental Divide. We carried everything we needed on our backs. At a place called Cirque of the Towers, we camped for three days in a basin flanked by vertical pink granite spires and carpeted with wild flowers. On the last day we added one more adventure to the others our expedition had given birth to. We scrambled up the talus slope under one part of the magnificently imposing escarpment, an approach that looked like it might yield passage to amateurs like ourselves. Paul led the pitches expertly, adroitly, pulling me along behind him. Breathlessly, we reached the high ridge and looked out over the whole expanse of the range to the north. Ridge after ridge, cloud-bannered peak after peak, snow still clinging in August to shaded north slopes, the Wind River Range stretched out gloriously before us. I've got a photo in my album, made with a self-timer, of the two of us, grinning as big as ever we've grinned. We were as proud of our achievement as anyone standing on the summit of Everest.

When he was a teenager, Paul had been fascinated with mountains, their lure and lore. He read all the books he could find about mountaineering. Posters from Rocky Mountain and Grand Teton National Parks and Ansel Adams' crisp Sierra photos papered the walls. It was a passionate attachment. He could talk for hours about the great peaks and climbers of the world. As happens to us all though, the responsibilities of making a living and raising a family gradually took all his time. The obsession had finally eroded to a hobby for which nowadays he had so little time. But Paul was a man who took his dreams seriously. The grief that withered his spirit and the outrage that muffled his passion were also a mourning, a lament for this unrealized vision of living to the fullest, which I know we shared deeply. I am sure he still dreams of mountain exploits. But somehow he never had ample opportunity. The blood had never fairly sang in his veins, his body fervent in bright sweat. His young heart had never adequately been strained, pounded and tested out in the biting cold air. His courage, strength and discipline had never been adequately proofed out in the glittering high sunshine.

What Paul was after was not escape. His innate integrity would never allow him to dodge responsibilities, to flee his commitments and struggles. Rather, I believe he sought the simple wholeness that comes from some kind of intimate and ongoing connection with the mysterious movements of life and nature, the genuine tides and rhythms of living, its waxings and wanings, ebb and flow, its sowings and harvests. There was a yearning ache in him that no medication from the pharmacy could ever relieve.

Paul just wanted to connect — honestly and wholeheartedly — with a magnificent and sacred world.

Now his best energies were spent meeting the challenges of daily living, the endless Monday through Friday campaign to keep up with both car payments and the kids' dental bills. The constant abrasions, the nettlesome noise, the revved-up treadmills siphoned off his strength, fractured during the week whatever serenity he could muster up on Sunday afternoon. The silver vampires of worry and care drained him constantly, undermining Monday's buoyant schemes, until Saturday promised some relief. A few weeks ago his house had been broken into, some property stolen. If it wasn't one damned thing, it was another.

Just before our evening together, Paul had even gone back to church, and he was continuing to attend, taking his kids with him. But he wasn't really finding what he wanted there either. He said he was somewhat tired of the same Bible stories over and over, and, what's more, they talked there of connections with holiness that seemed to Paul far-off and located in some future existence. He wanted more.

By now the news program on the TV had ended. A police show had taken its place. The silent screen reflected various hues of light out into the darkened room where we sat. During a pause in the conversation we stared at the screen. A fistfight on a city rooftop ended with the miscreant falling spectacularly to his death in the alleyway below. His fall was photographed in ravishing detail. Too late the police arrived, guns drawn. The victor perched on the edge of the roof looking down, dismayed. This tableau froze on the screen, the hoop and holler were over; the scene faded slowly into a commercial.

"Something is missing," wrote Protestant minister Renita Weems, "something inarticulate, yet conspicuous: Something ancient and precious; something so basic to our survival that its absence left us dazed. It's been missing for so long, we've forgotten its name."

Paul, it seemed to me, longed for the chance to have a real spiritual life. He wanted that combination of inner and outer adventures, those stout, enduring connections with the world that come when we care for our souls. This need is as basic to our nature as the urge for food or sex. The human family yearns for glimpses of the holy. We need to praise. We need to reverence. We need to serve others. We cannot live for long without those sensuous, yummy chills down the soul's spine that signal our sense of wonder has been satisfied. Lately we seem to have mostly forgotten the importance of all this. Without stout, enduring inward and outward connections with those we love, and without spirituality, there is a void inside. We feel empty and restless. We feel as though we are missing out on something crucial.

So we get up and turn on the TV. There, stylishly dressed Vanna White beams, prances and smiles, pointing coyly at the array of stuff on stage framed with blinking lights, soundtracked with upbeat brassy music and applause. A panoply of treasures beckons: shiny cars, polished furniture, gleaming appliances, elegant clothes, lavish cruises in the Caribbean. For a time these things fill that ache and vacancy. But it never lasts. All too soon we are uneasy and empty again. Anxiety and dread once again prowl our innards like hungry, sharp-clawed cats.

Spirituality is connection. Soul-making and the spiritual life are all about the ability to make linkages, breaking down the barriers that keep us at a distance from our deep desires for contact with a sacred world. Spirituality is expressed in the eloquent language of the world's great religions, but it is also found and nurtured when we participate in the most humble of daily activities. A spirituality that feeds our souls and heals our wounds is one that connects us with the beauty, the enchantment, the sacredness that lies everywhere we look in our own experience, that soaks everything in the world around us. Spirituality is making connections.

The Discontinuum Kitchen

Once I interviewed Gloria Davis in Santa Fe, New Mexico. She is Navajo and a Catholic sister. She talked at length about growing up in the midst of the austerities of the desert Southwest, in profound poverty, but in a community and culture that had not, like ours, severed most of its connections with a sacred world. She described her childhood as ongoing adventures and excitement in the midst of an enchanted landscape. She lived in a land that was considered alive; the mesas and canyons spoke to her people. The scarlet light of sundown and the various ways it rains, the rhythms and turnings of the seasons were named and honored. The Navajo relation to God is so fundamental that there is no word for "religion" in the language. Signs of the divine are perceived in everyday events, in illnesses, in the coming and going of animals, in the waxing and waning of springs. I remember feeling a profound envy of a culture in which the awe, wonder and sense of sacredness that every child carries with him or her is so validated, nurtured and celebrated.

Franciscan Father Richard Rohr tells this story from his life in the New Jerusalem lay community. A young couple in the community had just brought home a new baby brother for their four-year-old Tommy. They put the baby in his new crib; then Tommy asked if he could speak with the newborn alone. The couple hesitated for a moment, then agreed, but they eavesdropped through the bedroom door on this conversation. What they heard Tommy say was this: "Quick, Christopher, tell me who I am — tell me who God is — because I'm starting to forget!"

At a Midwestern conference on pastoral ministry I attended some years ago, the keynote speaker illustrated his talk about today's church with a slide, projected at great magnification behind him. Somewhere in the suburbs of Chicago a church community had taken the altar rail that had languished in the cellars since the renewal of Vatican II and had placed it on the front facade of the church itself. The intent was to show that the sanctuary of this church included all the people of God, each and every one of the parishioners. This is indeed a step in the right direction, but I submit that the altar rail should go round the whole planet, the whole universe. The interconnections are that widespread, far-flung and enduring.

Creation reveals God. For that reason alone it is sacred. Many theologians are saying today that the natural world is the primary revelation of God, that the Earth, for example, is the very body of God. Physicist Heinz Pagels maintains that the whole universe is a message written in code, and as such is revelatory of God. Ecopsychologist Theodore Roszak writes: "The natural realm is infused with divinity; to break faith with it is not only sacrilegious but crazy."

What surely will be judged the great sin of our age — the systematic destruction of the natural world — is also the step-by-step obliteration of the cradle that births our sense of wonder and ultimately the thoughtless massacre of our religious imagination and sensibility. Abysmally disconnected from the sacredness that is in the world, we make poor decisions, we blunder into irreversible mistakes. The current alarm and debate over the drastic climate change predicted as a result of global warming or the destructive hole in the protective ozone layer of our upper atmosphere are good examples. We overheat the planet and lacerate its skin. The rain forests, the very lungs of the world, disappear in a huge holocaust of greed. In our discontinuum kitchen, we squander the heritage that should be passed on intact to our young.

Is it any wonder our young are deeply troubled?

Emerald City Blues

What follows is the refrain from a popular song out of the "grunge" genre of popular music, widely listened to by teens and college-age youth these days.

> I'm sick of madams and misses.
> The only kiss for me

Is the kiss of the knife.
There's nothing on earth
That I'm not through with.
What can I do with
The rest of my life?

The world weariness and despair in those lines served up and sung by a young person today make the blood run chill. Here's Jody and his brother Cal, twenty-somethings out of a short story by a trendy noir writer, John Shirley Black. Jody is explaining to Cal how things are, thusly:

There's two things in the world, dude. There's making it like Marky Mark, like Eddie Murphy — that's one thing. You're on a screen, you're on videos and CDs. Or there's shit. That's the other thing. There's being huge and being nothing.

Nothing between glitzy fame and impotent insignificance? There's sadness beyond telling here in realizing that we have created the bulk and weight of a society which continues to provide, for millions of our young especially, a truly meaningless life experience. Occasionally I see a bumper sticker, usually stuck on the back of one of those road-hogging recreational juggernauts, that reads, "We're Spending Our Kids' Inheritance!" It's supposed to be snide, or cute, I guess, but this sentiment could well become a motto for the whole globe. The future looks increasingly strange, uncomfortable and alien to our young. The dream of ever burgeoning material progress has turned false. Young people seem to sense this intuitively. They are the ones who need to look to the future with more than just curiosity. Matthew Fox writes:

It is the young who have most of the nightmares about the future of this planet.... They are not in denial; they cannot afford to be. They know what is going on, what is happening to them and around them. Many are in the dark night of the soul, and that is not a bad place to be right now.

What drains us — especially the young — of enthusiasm and hope? From what hidden coffins do the bloodthirsty, pallid vampires of cynicism and despair slouch forth to feed on the best that is in us? Violence, crime, injustice, mayhem in our morality, politicians out of touch with the nation's real needs are just the usual suspects. Underlying these symptoms, is there not a widespread shriveling of the sense of wonder, a meagerness of the very thing that brings verve and joy, adventure and creativity to our living? Life has always been difficult. The grit, spunk, uncommon grace, humor, gusto and panache it takes to rise to life's challenges, it seems, are in ever shorter supply.

In working with young people on a daily basis, Robert Ludwig, director of university ministry at DePaul University in Chicago, detects an urgent spiritual hungering. "I hear," he said in an interview in *Praying*, "a need for some *personal* contact with the deeper mysteries and undercurrents of life. Young folks want to know they can connect their lives with things that really mean something and also make a difference." He identifies this spiritual hunger as a motivation for much drug use and sexual experimentation. Ludwig believes that we must hook our religions back up to their base in personal religious experience. At DePaul, on an ongoing basis, some 1,300 young people are involved in community service: tutoring children in housing projects, working with day care centers, with Habitat for Humanity, caring for crack babies in the inner-city, spending vacations at a rural ecology center. "They love it," says Ludwig. "When they graduate, some of our students talk about how this was the most profound experience of their education."

The young in particular need to be offered adventures, challenges against which they can match the best that is in them. Such challenges can be found in outer efforts or in inner spiritual strivings, in mind, heart and body adventures that enable them to make connections between their lives and others, and with something other. Adventures call on the potent magic that abides within each of us; in them there is always the hope of discoveries. Adventures have a way of sparking enthusiasm and building discipline, of cultivating achievement, of maturing us, then making us great souls.

Adventure and the sense of wonder, as every child knows, are intimately connected. They're best friends. They walk everywhere hand in hand. And they are the life forces that support, nourish and energize our spiritualities.

Vaclav Havel, playwright and president of the Czech Republic, draws similar conclusions about spirituality's demise. In his book *Living in Truth* he describes walking through the fields near his boyhood home in one of the most severely polluted parts of Eastern Europe and seeing the ugly, belching smokestacks of a factory nearby. He reflects:

> To me, personally, the smokestack soiling the heavens is not just a regrettable lapse of technology that failed to include the "ecological factor" into its calculations, one which can be easily corrected with the appropriate filter.... It is a symbol of an epoch which denies the importance of personal experience — including the experience of mystery and of the absolute — and displaces the personally experienced absolute as the measure of the world with a new, man-made absolute, devoid of mystery, free of the whims of subjectivity, and, as such, impersonal and inhuman.

What this artist-politician calls "the personally experienced absolute" is nothing less than a cosmos-connected spirituality, that place in each one of us where our hungering hearts meet up, by means of our connections to all creation, with the whisperings of divine glory and mystery. He is talking about personal religious experiences of God's beauty and mystery found in the world around us, not just in religion that is predigested, processed, packaged and hanging on the racks.

Just one very modest example is that intimate shiver you get when you stand in a clover field on a clear spring night and look up at the glories above. Another is Thomas Merton's famous encounter on a street corner in Louisville, when the faces of the passersby collectively glowed with the most tender radiance. These moments come to all of us. These experiences did not cease thousands of years ago when the last scriptural persona passed from the world.

Spirituality is born out of such personal experiences and thrives in our communities when we know we live in a richly sacred cosmos. The word *religion* itself means "to bind back to our origins." Such a cosmos-connected spirituality makes us adventuresome, because we know that divinity can be encountered almost anywhere. Wonder, awe, mysticism, joy, childlikeness, outgoing hearts, generosity, play and art are all welcome. Such a spirituality nourishes the heart and soul.

When smokestacks belch foulness that besmirches the very rain, when the great forests of the world are incinerated in order to serve up cheap hamburgers, so is our best humanity consumed in a conflagration of triviality, greed and stupidity. When the sense of wonder shrinks, our hearts burn like the forests. Havel declares that spirituality must be "the measure of the world," for only when we know we live in the midst of a sacred cosmos, the most holy of planets, will we able to summon the zest, perseverance and wisdom to preserve our little corner and to flourish as humans within it.

The Flesh of God is Compound Eye

Christianity is first and foremost an incarnational religion. That means that this faith tradition is centered on the divine enfleshed, alive and active within the ten thousand things of our world. In theology classes everywhere, students are taught that the Christian God is one who is experienced both as transcendent (wholly other, completely beyond our experience, our knowing) and at the same time as immanent (present, incarnate within creation). For centuries the emphasis in Christianity has been on the transcendent side. It is time for a change. The dilemmas and challenges we now face demand it. Religion that is entirely other-worldly, disembodied and disconnected is simply no help to us now, other than as some kind of escape. We desperately need spirituality that is this-worldly, embodied and connected. Such a spirituality is not grounded in pantheism, but rather in pan-en-theism, "God in things," where the deity's very flesh is compound eye, in a Spirit that whispers to us and is revealed everywhere — in beauty, in struggle, in species that are rapidly becoming extinct, in faces of our loved ones.

The late Father Bede Griffiths put it this way: "If Christianity cannot recover its mystical tradition and teach it, then it should simply fold up and go out of business; it has nothing to offer." The mystical tradition in Christianity is an ancient one, much neglected in recent centuries, though it has always been a nourishing river within. It has always proclaimed that creation is a wholeness, one that cannot be divided into parts. Creation is a seamless garment, a living and creative web of being. Everything is profoundly and deeply interconnected. Hildegard of Bingen said it 800 years ago: "Everything that is in the heavens, on the earth, or under the earth is penetrated with connected-ness, full of relatedness." This mystical tradition continued through the middle ages and beyond, in such persons as St. John of the Cross and St. Teresa of Avila. Twentieth century mystics, people like Simone Weil, Thomas Merton, John Shea, Annie Dillard, Macrina Wiederkehr, Ed Hays, continue the tradition.

Now as we begin a new century, modern science has joined with mystics from all the world's spiritual traditions in emphasizing that the cosmos we live in is indeed a wholeness, an interconnected web that cannot be separated or divided into discreet parts. The discoveries of relativity and quantum physics in our time especially underscore the profound unity and seamlessness of this world. Some physicists now maintain that the whole universe is dynamically implied and, in a sense, hidden, contained or enfolded into any of its parts, in what is called an "implicate order." The universe is a completely undivided and seamless whole — even the "objective" observer cannot be separated out from it.

Four centuries ago Galileo first peered through his inch-wide optical at the starry heavens. Since then our knowledge of the facts of life in the universe around us has grown, especially in the last two centuries. We now know for sure that the cosmos is a gargantuan-big place. Its size and complexity dwarfs all human experience. Also, we know that creation evolves, from simplicity to expanding complexity. We are part of an ongoing rather than static process. Instead of a system etched in stone, it is a rolling, flowing stream. God authored a cosmos that is sacred, most holy. With hard chalkboard theorems and quantum mechanics, science demonstrates the most elegantly subtle and thoroughly ingenious interconnectedness everywhere it looks — from subatomic particle to brain cortex to galaxy. Science has also revealed to us the holy history, the slow evolving of life, that over eons brought us here.

We are not only online with this holiness, we, each and every one of us (not just those who wear special collars and robes) live smack dab, lock, stock and barrel in its midst. The universe, as revealer of God, is sacrament. All its work is sacramental. The altar rail circles the universe.

Science itself is a kind of shrewd honesty, one that wants to know what's going on, how the world works. Recent discoveries in science, these great intellectual achievements of the last centuries, describe a universe which is much more like mind or a vast dance than it is like a machine. Yet for centuries the machine view of the world has dominated our thinking. In the eighteenth century, Sir Isaac Newton described the universe as a clockwork mechanism, set in motion by God, in which the cogs of things turn against each other mindlessly and planets circle stars in fixed, never-changing orbits. Cause and effect are separate entities, and they explain everything — period. Heat a certain amount of water to a certain temperature for a certain time and it will boil. Do it again the same way, same results. And on and on. This vast enterprise is devoid of intrinsic creativity and direction.

The great theologian St. Thomas Aquinas said, "A mistake about the universe results in a mistake about God." This machine view of the universe was simply a mistaken one, based on inadequate knowledge. Our view of things now is much better informed and refined, but it has yet to filter down, spread and widely influence our religious views. The old machine view has greatly contributed to the overemphasis on the transcendence of God, at the expense of clearly seeing and knowing God as involved and engaged in every aspect of creation.

"Because we are stuck in this view of the universe as a lifeless machine," said Father Diarmuid O'Murchu in a *Praying* interview, "we feel a deep sense of cosmic homelessness. The tragedy and scandal here are that this homelessness alienates us not only from the vibrant, creative universe we live in, but even from our own most intimate inner life, from our true self." Father O'Murchu points out that the only discipline now that recognizes and explores this connection between cosmic homelessness and our inner desolation is one that is quite new. It is the emerging field of ecopsychology (sketched out for the first time in Theodore Roszak's book *The Voice of the Earth)*. The ecopsychologist asks: "How can you have healthy people living on a dying planet? Does it make much sense to aspire to health in the individual when his or her surrounding and sustaining environment is on the decline in every way?" Ecopsychology emphasizes the interconnectedness of the human psyche with all the rest of life. O'Murchu says:

> A lot of mental illness and the huge amount of stresses we suffer as humans are because of what we are doing to the planet, because of the ongoing destruction of the environment. Until we begin a new relationship with the cosmos around us, we can't know how to relate meaningfully to anything, especially to our own innermost being. Without this meaningful relationship be-tween humans and the earth, the planet suffers profoundly and so do we suffer grievously, both physically and in our psyches as well.

The emerging field of ecopsychology is just one sign in our times showing that this old, tired-out view of our world as a machine, one that has been so busy separating, dividing and conquering, is slowly begin-

ning to yield to another view: one that knows that all things "inter-are."
We are beginning to reconnect.

The Universe Is as Mystical as the Great White Whale

This book then is about making connections. Connecting is, I
submit, a characteristic activity of a living, breathing, engaged and
passionate spirituality. This book is about making these connections in
a world that is alive with spirit, saturated with sacredness, shot through
and through with glory and deep mystery. This book is about the
daybreak within that occurs when we let the realization sink in that the
divine works within us, within all things, and that our living is truly
sacred adventure.

I opened this discussion with a description of my evening with
Paul because I think what Paul was after are the deep connections that
characterize an engaged and passionate spirituality. Paul had noticed
from childhood that the Earth he inhabits is a very remarkable place. His
love for mountains nourished that lifelong contemplation. In the peak-
littered landscapes he cherished, Paul saw that high-spirited energies
heave up shaggy, moonstruck and awesome places. He had witnessed
that the Earth is a place of blessing, extravagance and roughshod beauty.
Rootless and exiled spirits within Paul, full of imagination, deep longings and curiosities, met an outmatchingly muscular and heartily large
and promiscuous landscape without. Paul knew that enduring connections must be made between these two geographies, between the outside
and the inside. Spirituality is all about these kinds of connections.

We are called to be mystics, each and every one of us. What does
it look like to be a mystic? Here's my list of some characteristics:

The mystic celebrates relationality. The universe and planet
from which we come are woven-together fabrics, made of interconnections, mutual dependencies and relationships. We exist in the
midst of a living web. So the mystic sees, for example, making love as
a mutual and often sacred experience. The mystic knows the necessity
of friendship, of the acceptance of brokenness and loss, of maintaining
some kind of intimacy with the natural world that can teach us spiritual
lessons. The mystic trusts that since life is indeed a complex web of
interconnections, that nothing is ever really lost. Ultimately, every difficulty is an opportunity. These are some of the ways to love and live

relationality. It's a way of living that makes room for endless creativity, bottomless hope.

The mystic is tough and soft at the same time. Tough in the sense that she does not deny pain, suffering and death, never seeks refuge in sentimentality, magic or hooey. The mystic holds a faith in life itself, one that can exist beyond despair. The mystic is soft when he nourishes a tender compassion toward all things and continues to love the silences, the dirt under the fingernails, the tangy bite of a fresh apple, the homely pasture roses, the sweet tiredness of the body after hard work, the bony shoulders of the poorest, the smell of cabbage and carrots simmering on the stove. The mystic probably goes to some trouble to free the trapped moth in the window, yet is not overly concerned about her own comfort and convenience. The mystic lives imaginatively in the tension that exists between opposites.

The mystic cultivates his or her inner life and knows that the interior life exists not for his or her sake, but for the sake of the whole human community, for the whole planet. "What have you ever traveled toward more than your own safety?" asks Lucille Clifton. The mystic locates those fires inside that burn in outrage at the injustices in the world. The mystic spends time with those passions inside that lust and thirst for beauty, equality and wholeness restored to a broken world. The mystic does more than just navel gaze; she is active. She writes her congresspeople. She registers voters. She volunteers at soup kitchens. She organizes her neighborhood to buy from local organic farmers. She tutors high school kids who are having learning difficulties. In short, she makes connections between her inner stirrings and shiftings and the work that so urgently needs to be done outside, in her neighborhood, community and bioregion. Her life is a wondrous braid.

The mystic believes deep down that it is, after all, okay to be human. We humans sin. We're often afflicted with stupidity and the most appalling shortsightedness. We are indeed capable of monstrous personal, systemic and societal evils. We are in constant need of redemption and renewal. Yet at the same time, it is through and by means of the sufferings, deficiencies and limitations of being human that compassion is attained. We are capable of miraculous self-sacrifice. We can love one another deeply, passionately and playfully. We are able to create the most wondrous beauty and poetry, dance and music.

The facility to hope and dream is ours, by which we sustain ourselves in the cold and dark. As we learn, who knows but in the end we shall be wise enough to live someday in the goodness of which we are capable. After all, we're the wingless ones who can learn to fly, high as birds, in the golden balloon of our aspirations.

The mystic is enchanted by the world. Father Thomas Berry was once asked about the most important quality in the spiritual life, and he answered right back: "Enchantment." The mystic becomes enthralled by common things: the taste of ginger, the textures of leaves, the shapes of clouds, the sound of soft rains, the aroma of fresh-baked bread, the tang and bite of a crisp apple or the peaceful, holy darkness at night. The mystic can be ensorcelled by life's generous bounty: the voluptuous sadnesses of Mozart's slow movements, the huge bloody but miraculous mess of child-birth, the passionate orchestra of summer crickets, the lush disharmonies of Duke Ellington's arrangements, the poetry of Pablo Neruda or e.e. cummings, the moods of late autumn afternoons, morning light tingeing the treetops with soft gold, and on and on, world without end.

The mystic is thankful. A sense of thankfulness goes hand in hand with making connections, thankfulness for that long litany of enchantments that cast their spell over us day by day. Meister Eckhart, a thirteenth century mystic, said that if the only prayer you ever say is just a simple *thank you*, it will be enough. We have been given much and are expected to give in return.

Finally, **the mystic, the one whose life weaves and braids the sacredness of the world into itself, tries to notice, understand and call attention to the underlying connections that exist between disparate, separated things in our world**. For example, the mystic notices that our overemphasis on the light and accompanying pervasive fear of the dark might underlie much of the racism that continues to plague the world. Or, that our culture's avoidance of looking squarely at death in a forthright and honest way contributes greatly to our simultaneous fear of life, and perhaps to our continuation of a war machine that deals out death in a variety of ways, like selling land mines to third world countries. Or, that our refusal to value democratic principles as having a place in our homes and workplaces might contribute to the dwindling of democracy at the national level. Or, that human rights violations are closely connected to environmental degradation, as in countries like Nigeria where the military rulers sacrifice the health of whole villages to accommodate multinational oil companies and their money. This kind of connecting leads to deep insight and creative ways to solve problems in the world.

The mystic might even look at the bigger picture and see that at the center of the Earth there is a mother and probably at the center of our galaxy there is a dark void, but that's all right. Mothers and voids have a lot in common. Out of them come life, light and hope. There's a connection there.

The heart of this book is columns I have written in *Praying* magazine over the last six years. My column is named *Connections*. Each "connection" is a raid into the sacred world in which we live, or a celebration of that world, or perhaps just a snapshot, a glimpse, just a look at the way it is. Each is an attempt to name and describe, then spend some time with, the religious experiences each and every one of us has in our individual lives, all the time. One does not have to be ordained, vowed, specially garbed or appointed to encounter the sacred mystery of the divine.

There is in us a deep need for the sacred, for the experience of the divine among us and grounded in our hearts, a hunger that cannot be satisfied by theological statements or doctrinal proclamations. "Faith," wrote Carl Jung, "is no adequate substitute for inner experience." In the business and hurry, in the quiet moments, in our workplaces, in our meetings with others, in our attempts to solve problems, build better systems, think more clearly, act more decisively, in our play and in our rest, in our popular culture, in our politics and civic life, in every nook and cranny of our living, there is connection with the sacred.

The other day I gave Paul a call and we talked. He told me he had just turned down a promotion that meant more money but also more time away from his home. He along with his wife and boys were planning a backpacking trip together next summer, this time up in the high San Juans of Colorado. He and his wife were busy planning their route up through the Uncompahgre Wilderness. The two of them were busy sewing some new sleeping bags for the kids. The oldest boy was reading everything he could get his hands on about America's high wildernesses. Paul invited me along, asking me how long it had been since I had had a real adventure.

What Are Humans For?
Spirituality and Being Human

"There is nothing wrong with the human species today," says Matthew Fox, "except one thing, that we have lost the sense of the sacred." What does a society or world look like that has misplaced its radar for the sacred? Well, just look around, read the newspapers.

One primary symptom, I believe, is the way in which we have become experts at trivializing everything, at sucking the awe and mystery out of each and every aspect of our living. Guests on television talk shows display the most intimate details of their personal lives, sandwiched between ads for toilet bowl cleaners. Almost every seasonal day of celebration and rest is a lucrative bonanza of a marketing opportunity. Our politicians and civic leaders are now bought and paid for long before they get to the debate on key issues and public policies. We manage to pay quarterbacks and hockey goalies huge salaries, but somehow we can't find the money to repair our children's schools, pay teachers a decent wage or even allow little mom 'n' pop stores to remain in our neighborhoods. We hang on every detail of the life of a celebrity and simultaneously disparage our own living to the point that depression and low self-esteem are epidemic. We overrate the trivial, the frivolous and the glamorous at the expense of the best of our humanity, all the things that are really worth caring about.

Local life and communities everywhere are being discomforted, disrupted, endangered or destroyed. Our affluence buys us precious little joy. Speed, dissatisfaction and anxiety are our constant afflictions. "Road rage" spreads as we spend way too much time in our autos. We are all becoming helplessly dependent on distant markets and on a national economy that is alienated from us and which undernourishes us as we, unweaned, suck on its consumerist teats. We are dismembered from our work. Our leisure fails to renew us. The national motto has become, "Thank God, it's Friday!" These are all symptoms of the deepest soul devastation.

Healing perhaps begins at home: finding ways that are practical, available to everyone, rooted in age-old human practices that provide for the safekeeping of the small acreages the universe has entrusted to us. Block by block, household by household, one person at a time, may very well be the only way back to a world that is cherished as sacred.

Poet and farmer Wendell Berry wrote a wonderful book titled *What Are People For?* In it he asks pertinent, probing questions: Do communities and neighborhoods have a spiritual value? What is the proper relationship between the scale of human enterprise and the estate of nature? Berry was the keynote speaker at a conference I attended once. After his address, he introduced to the assembly an Amish farmer he had brought with him. This man was particularly eloquent, describing life on their human-scale farms in Pennsylvania. During the question-and-answer period, someone asked him what these farm people did in the winter when the crops had been harvested and snow covered the fields. "We take a lot of naps," he replied, and his answer got a standing ovation! That's how hard naps are to come by in our overachieving, time-stressed world! What really appealed to the crowd though, I believe, was the *human scale* of the Amish enterprise. The farmer talked of halting a communal plowing to move a meadowlark's nest from the path of their horse-drawn machinery. Profits were not the bottom line. Community and neighborliness took first place — and leaving plenty of room for human things, like quilting, putting up preserves, playing horseshoes, talking, eating together and napping, to name a few.

For too long, we have separated sacred and secular, relegating the sacred to certain places and certain people, while naming everything else as secular and devoid of the touch of divinity. In doing this we have profoundly devalued our own humanity. The truth is that divinity is constantly being revealed. It is revealed in the Scriptures, but it is also revealed in the sun, moon, stars, galaxies, in the sighing wind through the pine trees of a wilderness, in the face of your beloved, in the laughter of children. In Catholic grade school one of the first catechism lessons instructed us that we human beings were *made in the image and likeness of God*. What does that mean? Well, when you look into a mirror, your old familiar face stares back at you. When God looks into a creature, She sees Herself. That's what it means to be an image of God.

What are the implications of being an image of God? Well, for one, I think it means that divinity flows through and is revealed within our best human activities and enterprises. Our friendships, our family relationships, our sexuality, our childrearing, our intimate conversations, our attempts at courage, earth-restoring and justice-making, our coming together politically, our art, our music, our merrymaking, our efforts to heal one another, our best adventures of the mind, all of these human activities essentially reveal God. They are glistening, glittering mirrors. The ecstasy of lovemaking, the deep satisfaction that comes from effectively mentoring a young person, the "Aha!" moments of intellectual discovery, the soaking in mystery at the heart of our confrontations with pain and death, these are each and every one flat-out encounters with the sacred.

"Our souls are growing," says Matthew Fox. "They're not here to just keep clean and turn in at the end of our lives. We're here to grow, to grow our souls." Growing a soul is the best work there is. It happens when we undergo life's mysteries, steep ourselves in its wonders and delights, squarely and forthrightly face its challenges and dilemmas, strenuously work to reach out to others — especially the poor and marginalized — in compassion and solidarity, sweat to build better households, communities and institutions, or campaign to heal the wounded planet on which we live. Our souls grow when we are most deeply human.

Somehow we manage to both disparage our humanity and exalt it at the same time. We are told by TV evangelists that we are unworthy, abject sinners. Low self-esteem and depression are epidemic. There is widespread interest in angels and otherworldly creatures — beings that will perhaps save us from ourselves. We don't really feel good about our humanness; we're always trying to improve ourselves. Yet, at the same time, our human-centered theologies zero in on the relationship between God and the human — to the exclusion of all else. The nonhuman world seldom enters into our deliberations about our economic future or our speculation about our place in the divine scheme of redemption. We exclude ourselves almost completely from what Thomas Berry calls "the great conversation," that ongoing dialogue between us and our planet's rivers, mountains and forests. The rich resources of the natural world are seen as plunder, nothing more than the raw material that fuels our constant "progress." We see ourselves as the center of things, the last word on the subject of life forms.

In a tape program, Father Richard Rohr once said that what healthy spirituality should do, among other things, is leave us with a *proper* estimation of our value as humans, one that is neither too disparaging nor too exalted. Spirituality enables us to form a realistic measure of our value as humans. We need to hurry up and achieve this true measure, for a distorted and out-of-balance assessment of our humanity is truly destroying the planet. In the words of a leading environmentalist, Dave Foreman: "If we picture life as one of those great American chestnut trees just spreading thousands and thousands of branches out — if we see that as the tree of life — then we aren't just snapping off a few twigs out on the end of branches that may grow back in other ways. What we're doing is taking a chain saw to huge limbs of that tree of life." We casually destroy the other life with which we share the planet, with no sure knowledge of the consequences of such drastic tampering. And in our drive to improve ourselves, when bookstore shelves overflow with self-help tomes and new health regimens, do we ever stop to ask: What sense does it make to be a healthy person living on a dying Earth?

We are inhabitants of a planet; we share it with other life, rich and diverse. Our humanity is most holy. It follows from these two assertions that our farms, our neighborhoods, our towns and cities, our marriages, our parenthood, our neighborliness, our efforts to build a better world together, our work, these are all places where the sacred is revealed. Some of the values that accompany such assertions are these: simplicity, stewardship, dialogue with the land, fidelity to place, the ability to consecrate the ups and downs of life, a contemplative and mystical spirituality. These are the virtues for a new century and a new millennium, when we will — at last, perhaps — figure out what humans are for.

Get a Life!

Steven Spielberg, the film maker whose credits include such block-busters as *ET*, *Schindler's List*, *The Color Purple*, *Jurassic Park* and *Amistad,* was being interviewed. A critic had panned his films because of excessive references to other movies. Speilberg's reply: "Of course, he's right. That's all I know. I grew up in the suburbs and all I ever did was watch movies. Then I started making them. I never had a life."

He spoke of his admiration for Hollywood director John Huston, who made such cinema masterpieces as *The African Queen*, *The Maltese Falcon* and *The Treasure of the Sierra Madre*. Speilberg noted Huston had worked variously as a longshoreman, a roustabout in the Southwest oil fields and even a stint as a bouncer in a Mexican brothel. He had a wide experience of life under his belt. Speilberg felt this showed up in spades in his film work. Huston's movies stood on their own — redolent with evocative mood and inventive camera work — and too busy telling a whopper of a tale to have time to refer to other films.

Teenagers, those perennial fonts of wisdom, often express themselves in insightful cliches. One of my favorites is the exhortation, "Get a life!" It's good advice, especially for those concerned about integrating spirituality into everyday living. We've inherited a point of view from the past that is too otherworldly, disembodied. In our religious sense there's a split between the spirit and flesh, sacred and secular, heaven and earth. It's probably a big reason why we trash the planet like we do.

Our popular image of a holy person has been someone withdrawn from the world, a loincloth-clad guru meditating alone in a cave, a monk cloistered away in silence. But this image is changing to that of a person hip-deep in reality with her sleeves rolled up: a social worker surrounded by a city's homeless, a volunteer slain by death squads in the middle of Central American poverty, a nun mopping the brow of a dying sidewalk-dweller in Calcutta, a protestor disabling a nuclear missile silo in the Midwest. These are people who not only have a life, they are passionate about giving others the opportunity to have a life as well.

The life we live need not always be packed with toil and service. Pat Livingston, a sought-after speaker at ministry conferences, recalls the time she gave the keynote address at a New York City gathering. Afterwards in the reception line, a man asked her what she was going to do with her time in the Big Apple. "Prepare my next talk," she answered. "What?" he gasped. "You're smack in the center of world civilization with art galleries, museums, restaurants and theater that are all once-in-a-lifetime experiences (not to mention the chance to watch the sunset over the ocean from the top of the World Trade Building), and you're going to lock yourself up in a room with a speech!" Right, she thought, and out she went for a day on the town that would glow in the album of her memories.

Ed Hays, founder of the Shantivanam prayer community, asks us to think about the Rent-a-Wolf plan, an old bit of folk spiritual wisdom. This plan maintains that, if there is no wolf at your front door, you should hire one to come and howl. "Life is trouble, and trouble holds the magic to bring us together or destroy us," says Father Ed. "Troubles can bring forth greatness from us, heroism as well as creativity, or breed self-pity, bitterness and a host of other evils. When our work and life in general are going smoothly, how easily we tend to forget about others who are in need . . . . By sharing in the holy communion of trouble, we become bonded more tightly together as members of one great family."

Since life, as we all know, is usually a lot of trouble, it follows that in living one automatically reaps the benefits of Hays' Rent-a-Wolf plan. Every day we sit at the table where the holy communion of trouble is shared. If we could run off to meditate in a cave in the Himalayas, navel-gazing til the sacred cows come home, we'd confront few hassles, only washing out our loincloths from time to time, but we would also likely not make much spiritual progress. Our easily-won serenity would probably be shattered into pieces by the first wailing two-year-old or neurotic freeloading panhandler that shuffled our way.

Gloria Davis teaches Native American spirituality in New Mexico. Her notions about spirituality were formed growing up in her traditional Navajo family. "I noticed," she told me, "that the holy people in our community, the ones we turned to for spiritual guidance, who conducted the blessing and healing ceremonies, were always the people who had the keenest sense of humor. You could always tell them by their laugh wrinkles." What an idea! The hallmark of holiness here is not a gaunt, hollow-cheeked face or a look of otherworldly serenity, but just a common lively sense of humor. Surely a sharp funny bone has rarely been honed in a cave or cloister, but is made on the lathe of life's ups and downs, its absurdities and sorrows, its humdrums, its joys and comical interludes, its tedium, tensions and ironies, its unpredictable encounters and quiet satisfactions.

Meister Eckhart, medieval mystic, said that God is tickled pink when we manage in the midst of our difficult lives to show compassion, to do an unrewarded kindness for another. I like that image of the higher power. And I like that strategy for getting a life that is truly human and truly holy. So, make God smile. Be kind to one another. Make God laugh. Get a life!

Some Spending Money

One Monday morning the headlines in our local paper announced a stunning, shocking event. Dr. Marshall Saper, radio show psychologist, had killed himself. Every morning for years Dr. Saper had dispensed advice to the distraught and confused. His suicide pulled the rug from under a whole city's sanity. Grief, disbelief and dismay followed, along with speculation on how this man of good counsel had somehow been unable to sustain that courageous "dedication to reality," which is how one bestselling author and psychiatrist defines mental health.

Who can know another's soul or glimpse at the angels and demons that wrestle therein? However, I couldn't help thinking that, undergirding whatever other reasons Dr. Saper might have had to despair, there might well have been a mighty weariness of always being the "expert" to whom so many of us turned for advice and support. Did his own credentials fail him down in the nightmare burrows, the anguished arena of pain, darkness and bitter struggle we all must enter now and then?

Are we too dependent perhaps on our experts, our authorities? Every newspaper and magazine is packed with columns and articles dispensing information and advice on all manner of things: how to dress for success, how to cope with bad hair days, how to avoid toxic relationships, how to find peace of mind, how to slow down, how to speed up, how to become an expert yourself and cash in on those high consulting fees — all penned by the world's foremost authorities. We can't fall asleep without first getting charts and explanations of tomorrow's weather from local meteorologists. None but the brave will venture to the movies without consulting Siskel and Ebert. It may have been my imagination, but I swear some years ago when John Paul II was shot the networks immediately produced a bespectacled foremost authority on papal shootings to interpret the event for us. And as far as I know, this was the first time a pope had ever been shot!

We may be the most well-informed people that have ever drawn breath, but *are we very wise*? Agriculturist-philosopher and farmer Wes

Jackson reminds us that the most important information we possess is now disappearing faster than the free coffee at my 12-Step meetings, namely the species diversity and life forms it took the earth five billion years to craft. Unimaginably complex genetic information, honed and shaped by geological eons, so hard-won that literally billions of lives underwrite it, is all wiped out casually, without much thought, mowed down so that we can eat cheap hamburgers. Jackson suggests we pay this disappearing wealth of diverse information such little respect because of the illusion that knowledge overall is so plentiful on our computers, in the halls of academe. We snatch the latest info on stock prices or celebrity horoscopes off our modems while the ancient wisdom of the earth perishes an acre at a time, a species or two a day. "Our whole planet is being destroyed," says Father Richard Rohr, "by people with college diplomas."

What personal price do we pay for this overreliance on specialists, "advanced" knowledge and lofty degrees? I suspect it may also be in hugely underestimating, neglecting and failing to develop our own inner resources and wisdom, our well-nigh miraculous capacity for creativity, imaginative problem-solving and healing. Perhaps when God put us down here on earth, she put some spending money in our pockets.

Once not so long ago, most of us lived closer to the challenges of the land — as third world peoples still do. Danger, hardship, the demands of farming, hunting, human strife and extended families honed our resourcefulnesss, our wonderworking cleverness and our ordinary, everyday moxie. This knowledge too was hard-won, eked out in blood, sweat and tears. Another casualty of modern life seems to be that lusty confidence in our own inner wisdom, the savvy that comes from working things out when faced with huge difficulties. Farming and hunting are nearly gone; life's difficulties still abound.

I am not saying we don't need professionals, people who are highly skilled and knowledgeable about this or that. Brain surgeons and airline pilots come immediately to mind. But surely, in our current epidemic of low self-esteem and stress, we could greatly benefit from honoring and respecting the wise craft and artful expertise each of us has acquired negotiating the shoals and outsmarting the booby traps that plague every single life, no matter what our station or status.

Experts are hard to escape. Within me lurks that tiresome know-it-all, that cocksure voice which can't ever just leave a mystery alone or just simply shut up to bask in the goose-pimple awe and delicious wonder that surrounds the unthinkably vast, uncharted *terra incognita* of the continent of things I don't know, haven't a clue about. "That the world is unfathomable," said Vaclav Havel, "is part of its dramatic beauty and charm." I am tired of that guy inside me who has to explain everything all the time, who can't ever admit humble ignorance.

Herman Melville, author of *Moby Dick*, once gave this advice: "Don't expand your mind. Make it subtle!" How do we become wise and truly human? Let's neglect the experts, believe the good news, dig down in our pockets and find that spending money, then go out on a spree!

Comin' Atcha

Sometimes I think my old friend Emery was nothing less than a saint, one of those holy and sacred fools so honored in Eastern spirituality. My neighbor when I lived in the Missouri Ozarks, Emery oozed with life. His frisky sense of humor sat poised on a hair trigger. He took risks and often fell flat on his face. Emery had a rich inner architecture. He was blessed, an original, surprised you often, but was trustworthy and disciplined too. Emery was, as they used to say, a man of many parts.

When the most chuckleheaded buffoons endure way past their allotted fifteen minutes of fame, for me Emery was an antidote to this hucksterism and hornswaggle so pervasive in our time. His best qualities combined to make him a wonderful friend, a reliable companion for any chancy venture, voyage or trek. Someone once suggested this exercise: Imagine you must undertake a very difficult journey fraught with hazard and uncertainty, wherein the outcome was very much in doubt. Who among your friends or acquaintances would you want along as companions? Make a short list. Emery would be near the top of mine.

Emery looked lived-in. His self-cropped hair curled out from under the railroad caps he wore, summer and winter. Walking the Ozark hills and eating from his wife Serena's spacious garden kept him fit. Emery made his living as a carpenter and drove a '52 Ford pickup he called *Comin' Atcha*. It was primer-colored, sporting a homemade pine bed and oak rails in the back. When low on cash, he'd truck the hills looking for medicinal herbs to sell. He knew and loved the high ridges and wild things around Mad Dog Hollow, Skranky Knob and beyond.

A visit with Emery was always a joy. Emery built his house himself, a two-story structure sided with rough-cut oak. He covered the front with Ozark stone, capped it with a fluted, gabled roof shingled with handmade cedar shakes. Circled by dogwoods and mulberries, the house squatted under a swerve of the hillside below Skranky Knob. In April bloodroot and trillium carpeted the backyard. Stepping through the door was an adventure. Walls were panelled with native woods like persimmon or sassafras, retrieved from the local sawmill. High on shelves in the living room his woodcarvings sat in silent repose: flying squirrels, armadillos, spicebush caterpillars, coiled copperheads itching to strike, even a few outrageous-looking species he'd devised. My favorite was his rendition of the notorious Ozark woolly-booger, that denizen of the deepest woods who sometimes lurks outside cabin doors at midnight, seldom seen but sometimes glimpsed silhouetted against moonslivers. Besides whittling, Emery invented. Out in a corner of the barn a table was piled high with welded-together pipes, piano wire and retrieved parts from an old tower clock. If a Volkswagen mated with a Tibetan prayer wheel, with antique hairdryers and tube radios somewhere back in the family tree, their progeny would resemble this invention on which he was working, whose purpose was obscure.

In the house, books spilled off shelves into piles on the floors along the walls: from Edgar Rice Burrough's tales of Mars and Pellucidar, through *Moby Dick, Lord Jim, Nostromo, The Jungle Book,* to Frost and Shakespeare. He particularly liked mysteries, so he was loaded with Rex Stout, Ngaio Marsh, John D. McDonald. His music collection was also broad and good: the old guys like Doc Watson, Tubb and Cash, Miles and Monk; and the old gals: Piaf, Holiday, the Carters and Cline. Emery kept up too: He had Raitt, Te Kanawa, Springsteen and Clapton.

From the rafters hung herbs from both the garden and the dark woods to dry: mountain mint, sage, catnip, dill, basil and goldenseal. In the corner crouched an old telescope. On a board were arrayed snapshots of his two kids, Emery in among them in one with a sly, goofy grin, looking like Gyro Gearloose, wearing a beanie with a propeller atop it and thick coke-bottle-bottom hornrimmed glasses — gifts from his wife one long-gone birthday. A squeaky screen door led out to the long-roofed porch. Summer nights would find us sitting out there, heat lightning blazing far off in the distance, unmasking boiling cloud banks momentarily backlit. Upstairs his oldest would often be listening to the Cardinal's game, Jack Buck's voice droning out into the night, mixing with the summer hum of insects. We'd gossip about the neighbors. Then the talk would meander round to the summer's beauty, then to what might lurk behind that beauty.

Once we got a distress call from our friend Lee Grady up on Cheney Ridge: Lee's wife was hemorrhaging badly from a miscarriage.

We went to get Lee's kids so Serena could look after them for a few days. A nasty storm came on us fast from the southwest. With Lee's little girl and boy in the seat between us scared to death, *Comin' Atcha* bounced over the rough logging road across the tilting glades poised above steep ravines. Lightning splintered postoaks up above. The wind drove directly into us, whipping rain furiously against the windshield. Emery took up the beat of the wipers and began to sing: "Sal's got a meat rind hid away, to grease my wooden leg every day." Then, "Rattle up a ginseng, you can't jump josie." He finished with, "Jiggety-jiggety windy cup, how many fingers do I hold up?" and a chorus of "Iko-Iko." He had the kids and me laughing in no time.

We forget too easily what miracles we are! At our best we're like bubbling, brave, dazzling comets. No wonder God loves us! I confess to delight in full-bodied, juicy, quirky people, because they seem working definitions of what it means to be saintly, to be whole, to be responsibly free. They're living answers to the question, "What are humans for?" Henry Miller added this response: "To season one's destiny with the dust of one's folly, thereby releasing life's endless powers for healing, courage, ecstasy and merrymaking, that's the trick."

The Wizardry of Oz

Not long ago at a retreat I met Graeme visiting from New Zealand. At dinner he spoke of his distaste for the phrase "down under" to describe his home. "It's only down under," Graeme fumed, "because of the way maps are drafted. At home you can buy maps drawn with Australia and New Zealand on top and the U.S. and Europe on the bottom. It's pole-ism!"

Discussion turned to how our reality is shaped by the maps we draw and how we then mistake the maps for the reality. Astronauts report difficulty with orientation when circling the planet. It's hard to get used to a universe where there really is no up or down, no unmoving reference point from which to judge all the rest. We wound up affirming the importance of inclusive language and attention to our God-pronouns. Our conversation shed light as well on the question of mysticism, which is, after all, that aspect of religious activity that concerns experience. It is about exploring the actual territory, not about the maps.

An unforgettably haunting dream visited me in my twenties: With a small group of people I huddled outside the closed door of a mysterious room. Beyond the door in that room was something so unknown, so inexplicable, but so potent with coruscating energy, that we outside palpitated with a ribcage fear. That terror knifed past the dream barrier to soak my whole body in sweat and sent the hairs on the back of my neck reaching for the sky. In the dream, not one of us had the courage to open the door, for we somehow knew just a glimpse inside would shatter us into a million pieces. Was it some dread avalanche of glory, or an emissary from the very Face behind the veiled mask? Was it the Presence that drove stouter-than-oak, dark-opinioned Ahab mad as he dogged titanic Moby, trying to pierce that veil with his harpoon in the greatest of American novels? It was certainly a dream about the numinous. Rudolf Otto, in his important book about the basis of religion, *The Idea of the Holy,* identified such human experiences, naming them as encounters with the Mystery, tremendous and fascinating, the source and wellspring of human religion (not religiosity). You and I have these encounters. They didn't stop with Moses, Paul or even with Francis of Assisi.

Once at a moonlit picnic on a beach in northern California under the looming bulk of Mt. Tamalpais, friends (one of whom I was in love with) and I toasted hot dogs over a driftwood fire while a thick shroud of fog crouched over hissing surf glowing with humid luminescence. Between bouts of merriment, with the salty musk of stranded kelp blending with the incense of her red hair, I heard the faraway barking of seals out in the vast heaving darkness of the Pacific. So moondazzle intoxicated with life that night was I that at that moment I could not catch my breath. I might easily have fainted with sheer piss 'n' vinegar exultation had I not burnt my finger on a marshmallow. An opposite correlative was a moment several years ago, when my wife was in the throes of untreated mental illness, grotesque syllables hemorrhaging from her mouth like black blood during a manic siege. I was so bowel-wrung scared, daunted by the dark, senselessly unfair horror life can bring to good folks in the blink of an eye that I could not stand up. My skin crawled. My tongue dried out. The awful air was too moronic to breathe.

Deep draughts of the Mystery — such moments unshuck the soul, and they come to us all. *Religion is about the mystery of our lives.* Spirituality thrives when we know we live in a sacred world that crawls with evidence of the numinous. We have not just heard of it; we have tasted it, been both exalted and knocked loopy and dazed by it. Such a cosmos-connected spirituality makes us alive, awake and adventuresome because we know divinity (Father, Mother, Son, Spirit, a Glory that prompts praiseful alleluias, the Mute Unknowable before which we cry heartfelt sobbing pleas for mercy) can be encountered anywhere. Wonder, awe, humility, outgoing hearts, generosity, courage, ritual, play, art and prayer are the only ways to deal with the living Mystery we call God. Our religion should serve as container, map, counselor, not a substitute for this life of encounter.

I can understand why Father Tom Berry says the single most important spiritual quality is enchantment. No doubt every child's favorite parable about how enchantment works has been *The Wizard of Oz*. It's chockful with towering tornadoes, witches sporting striped socks, officious munchkins, fanged flying monkeys and bad puns. With its open-eyed gaze at aspects of nature that don't dance in goody two-shoes, some tots watch it stiff with fright. As every kid knows, the larger-than-life figures over the rainbow turn out to be the same people found at home, out in our backyard, in the neighborhood. When you know down in your joints and up in your straw-filled head that you live in a sacred cosmos, well, the ordinary is always extraordinary. The way to the Emerald City is an adventure-filled enterprise that tests our courage, compassion, steadfastness and wit — as good a definition of spirituality as any I've heard. Oz the Great and Powerful is revealed to be a bamboozling snake-oil salesman toying with smoke and mirrors. He's a mapmaker, not an explorer. Yet the quest is not in vain, for the real wizardry of Oz turns out to be the plain insight that our feet are shod with the magic of our heart's desire, always have been.

The ruby slippers are in the back of the closet, and the pearl of great price is down tangled in our pocket lint. Unless we become as little children, wide-eyed with healing enchantment, with the mystical dimension of our religious tradition, moving from a fearful life to a bold contributive one, crafting a heart down in the smithy of our soul, all the maps in the world will never get us back home. Unless we become immersed in the enchanting Mystery, we will never really know what humans are about — or for.

Pray, Tell Me More

Eavesdropping is a hobby of mine! On the bus, in a restaurant or waiting room, I confess to sometimes burying my head in a magazine, then listening in on others' conversations. You hear a lot. On a recent train trip, an older woman and a younger one who had just met talked in the seats behind me. For the elder (let's call her Ivy), it was a monologue with brief interruptions. Ivy was completely absorbed in herself, and whatever the younger woman (let's call her Viv) said would remind Ivy of something else about Ivy. After an hour or so, we knew more than we wished about Ivy, while she had learned precious little about Viv, a single mother who had wrestled her two kids down to a nap and was enjoying a rare moment's peace and who, when she got a word in edgewise, sounded as though she could have used an ear. When I passed Ivy later, she was looking out the window with the loneliest look on her face.

Listening is a kind of mindfulness. This simple act is almost Godlike. Brenda Ueland calls listening "a powerful, magnetic and strange thing, a creative force." She writes: "Think how the friends who really listen to us are the ones we move toward, and we want to sit in their radius as though it did us good, like ultraviolet rays." Listening to another validates that person's experience. All of us need the validation that comes from being listened to; it is absolutely essential to nourish and sustain that inner affirmation we call self-respect. Without such self-respect, we are shut up in the solitude of our own hearts. Indeed, our hearts are hungry to be listened to, to simply be noticed. How often do we hear children clamor, "Look at me! Mommy, Daddy, World Out There, look at me!" When we are listened to, well noticed, it creates us. It makes us unfold and expand. "We go home," says Ueland, "rested and lighthearted."

It actually takes great inner resources to be a good listener. Many of us feel that unless we are doing the talking, we are socially of no account. Only a mindful kind of self-possession and patient strength can allow one to listen well to others, just hear what another is saying, without jumping in with advice or changing the subject back to one's own concerns. It's almost a litmus test for progress in the spiritual life: How well can I listen?

It's a tin-eared world we live in now. Our elected leaders don't listen much to the electorate; they're too busy answering calls from corporate lobbyists or their big campaign contributors. This alienates us from politics so much that only a few vote. The media don't listen; they get blindsided almost weekly. Bosses don't listen much to workers, and it's reflected in poor decisions, thoughtless downsizing. Marriage counselors' appointment books bulge at the seams; "not listening" is the chief complaint when the partners arrive. In a New York minute, most of us are ready to proclaim our particular brand of victimhood to all and sundry, and the chorus of overlapping monologues is deafening. We all probably listen least well where we most need to — inside our own families, especially to our children.

Michael Nichols in his wonderful book *The Lost Art of Listening* describes the endless circle. One does not feel sufficiently heard. So one talks even more, maybe even compulsively. That drives others away, so one gets even less listening, ratcheting up the compulsion. Round and round it goes in ever-widening gyres, and where it stops . . . .

"I never knew you felt that way." "Pray, tell me more." "Thanks for listening." What power to short-circuit that circle! What magical phrases!

We don't even really listen well to ourselves. There is an untapped world of exploration, entertainment, purpose and renewal that has the potential to dwarf even the much-touted Internet. It is our own inner lives. Contemplatives everywhere always have counseled us to listen carefully to our own hearts, to our own innards, for as Jesus says, the kin-dom of God is within you (Luke 17: 21). This is why solitude is much touted in the spiritual life, for solitude is the opportunity to give ourselves, and God, a good listening to.

Here's a real spiritual exercise. Next time you're at a party, a lunch or family gathering, dedicate yourself that one afternoon or evening to just listening. When someone talks to you, try to pay attention without pressing your own mind against him/her, changing the subject or arguing. You will know you are succeeding if 1) you find yourself asking the person to whom you are listening questions about what he/

she is saying to you; **2)** the person to whom you are listening begins to bloom; **3)** after you are finished, the person to whom you listened shows a genuine interest in you and what you have to say. It's not easy, but it can be magically rewarding.

It's important to listen now and then to those who don't agree with us. On a recent train trip, I conversed with a fellow-traveler in the snack lounge. We could not have been more mismatched, by political views, by our inclinations in spirituality, by our dispositions in general. At first we bristled and snarled at each other, but somehow we remained tethered by some kind of mutual respect, or maybe just our mode of travel. My own beliefs were challenged, some of my arguments short-circuited, and I found the only way I could well defend my point of view was by descending into my heart. My antagonist did the same. It's so rare for men to have time and space to do this together, yet I believe it's time well spent. After several hours' conversation, though neither of us had changed our views, both of us, I think, had somehow achieved a more full-bodied, grounded, respectful stance.

What potent magic! Pray, tell me more.

Meeting Dejah Thoris

Spirituality writer Sam Keen once devised what he calls spiritual bullshit detectors. There is an array of questions one might ask of any spiritual tradition, movement or leader to which one is about to pledge allegiance. Does a spiritual authority, for example, offer a universal blueprint for salvation or a ready-made map of your spiritual pilgrimage? Avoid those who do. Does a group or leader demand you place loyalty to them higher than your loyalty to your mate or family? If so, run for your life. One that particularly delighted me: Does your guru have any friends? Check to see if a spiritual leader has peer relationships and a community of equals, or only disciples. Distrust anyone who claims to have achieved universal compassion but lacks the capacity for simple friendship. Friends keep us honest. Without them we simply cannot be whole.

If you had a long journey to undertake, one fraught with hardship and peril, and you could take two people along with you, whom would you choose? Your best friends perhaps. Maybe not so much for their aid while you taunt the sabertooth, dismantle the war machine, speak truth to Power or try to frame a wise reply to epithets and slack-jawed slaverings, but for all those soulful conversations and delightful pauses to chortle and guffaw which you could enjoy between your ordeals.

My top choice: John, my friend of nearly forty years, whom I first met in our high school library. It was a retreat day, and both of us had sought the shadowy solace of the fiction racks, searching for the latest spiritual reading from J.R.R. Tolkein or Lester Del Rey. We complemented each other neatly. John is imaginative, extroverted, a born storyteller. John lives in his senses, while I introvertedly dwell in my head. Both of us are book-lovers. That day John kindly introduced me to the escapades of the luscious Martian princess Dejah Thoris, later to Captain Nemo, to Fafhrd and the Grey Mouser, to the brooding Gormenghast trilogy and the thrilling quests of the *Lord of the Rings* series. After homework, we would stuff our eyes and feed our heads with this rich mulch for the imagination, with comics, pulp fiction and our own inventions: homespun fantastical tales, magical names, ribald farces and outlandish ghost stories.

Evenings when the windowpanes were frostbit and the popcorn popped, we'd play movie soundtracks and make up derring-do that featured the two of us valiantly rescuing our current heartthrobs from the clutches of evil villains whose mannerisms remarkably matched those of certain of our teachers.

Afloat on buoyant schemes, we ran to meet the promise of our future, to prop up the sky with our hurtling youth. Our journeys were perilous enough — the gauntlet of dating, the moral challenge of the Vietnam war, and all the other social tumults of the '60s. Together we opened the champagne jars of life, sent up some kites, chased our pretty thistle girls. Somehow we spun past all the needle hisses, raucous scratches and deep rents of our young lives to hear most of the soulful tunes intact. We pondered life's jolly-grim polarities, confusions and conundrums on many mockingbird-serenaded summer evening walks. From across the Rockies, Sierras and the Pacific, we wrote each other thick, tangled, typed-on-onionskin letters. Like most of us, we gyroscoped (don't ask me how!) through decades of tricky or trying times, our friendship like an often leaking but enduring rain barrel.

Partly due to my friend John, I live now as a man with a child — astir and sometimes sneaker-clad and running — inside of me. Thanks, friend.

There's more. John's personality fortissimos. He has abandoned promising bureaucratic careers to work in comic book stores. Once he quit a job, rented an office in a downtown skyscraper, installed a type-writer, taking six months off to live on cornflakes, and wrote a captivating novel about the misadventures of some elves. Enthralled by his bravado, I satellited in his sunshine too much for my own good, even trying to ape his stories, which I wasn't very good at. Awakening from this futility, I found and cultivated my own passions: my love for nature, for social-justice activism and for adventures of the mind. I learned to fill that cipher within me . . . with me. Lo and behold, on that quest for my heart of hearts, thanks to my friendship, I found myself better off, for my imagination had been stretched like candy at a taffy pull. I could summon to my endeavors badly needed whimsy and a richly endowed playfulness. Most helpful of all — a treasure trove, in fact —

has been that adventuresome, speculative, waltzin' across the galaxies, widest possible point of view characteristic of the imaginative literature in which John and I steeped ourselves between grass-cutting jobs.

This lifelong encounter of friendship has both enriched my world immeasurably and at the same time needled and prodded me into locating my own unique voice and point of view. A constant dance back and forth, it is the paradox of community and individuality, an insoluble puzzle we stew over for a lifetime. Thomas Moore writes: "It helps to soak our notion of friendship in this mystery: when I have opened my heart to a friend, I am more myself than ever."

Often I catch myself longing to be either a celebrity or some icon of purity or of politically correct selflessness. Falling short as I invariably do, I feel an abject failure. At last a flicker of wisdom dawns. I believe I'll aim for a more down-to-earth, commonplace goal: maybe just being a good friend to my friends. It's funny, but the more I invest myself in friendship, the more me there is to give — and the more human I become.

Somersaults and Tomfoolery

One of my favorite wise women, Brenda Ueland, once counseled parents exhausted by their energetic children, fed up with endless evening exhortations to get their children to bed, thusly:

> You yourself should be so vigorous, healthy, in the pink of condition, so inexhaustible, rambunctious, jolly, full of deviltry and frolic, of stories, of jokes and hilarity, of backward somersaults and tomfoolery, that your children at last, after hours of violent exercise, worn down by laughter and intellectual excitement, with pale, neurasthenic frowns on their forehead, cry: "Pleee . . . eease, Mama, go to bed!"

Hildegard of Bingen, twelfth century mystic, counseled her spiritual directees to be "juicy people," folks who are so filled with wonder and curiosity, with lusty appetites and high spirits, that they embrace life, liberty and the pursuit of happiness with a burly, grinning bear hug. To be juicy is to be: a fearlessly joyous optimist, a troublemaker tirelessly afflicting the comfortable, a passionate lover of good talk and tasty food, an anonymous prophet hovering over the cosmological riddle, a frequent violator of the ordinance against indecent exposure of the heart, and a guerilla in the insurrection against Dream Molesters everywhere. Mostly, juicy folk are starry-eyed trespassers on that wide boulevard Matthew Fox calls the *Via Positiva*. A deep well for our spirituality is to be found — *mirabile dictu!* — in all the good things of life. In awe, delight, enjoyment, pleasure, making friends with beauty, falling in love, being fascinated by the everyday wonders of the world around us, we sustain ourselves and fill our lives with adventures. Juicy people act as if they had just read a headline that shouts, "Scientists find universe is awash in tiny diamonds!"

The juiciest people in my life stand as my heroes and heroines. In their presence, I feel I'm walking on water. I'm enlarged by knowing them. And they seem empirical evidence of the truth of Henry Miller's statement: "If we have not found heaven within, then it is a certainty we won't find it without."

I already spoke of my juicy friend, John, who once took a year off and wrote a delightfully quirky page-turner of a novel about some elves and their high and low adventures, a fantasy which he'd been hankering to get on paper.

I also knew an older couple, owners of a sheep ranch outside Petaluma, California, who had spent their honeymoon long ago flying an open-cockpit Steerman biplane down the Central Valley, across the rugged Sierra foothills and arid Mojave, all the way to the tip of the Baja Peninsula, where they angled for swordfish. They navigated by means of gas-station road maps and, when dark came, landed in pastures, slept covered with wool blankets on the ground and cooked dinner on the engine coils of the Steerman. How I envy them those memories!

Another juicy friend is Christina. Passionate about archeology and seeing the world, she hitchhiked alone around the Middle East in the late '70s. Once I got a card from her with an Iranian postmark and a photo of the ruins of Persepolis, the city Alexander the Great built during his Persian conquest, wherein he ordered his officers to marry Persian women 2,500 years ago. She had slept in a moonlit cave near the ruins that night. Other postcards came from Lascaux in France and from the Valley of the Kings in Egypt. Juicy!

Being juicy, we run the risk of becoming anachronisms in a world that is getting smaller, meaner — and ever more homogenous. The way we're going, it won't be long before the farthest reaches of Tibet will resemble the cheesy outskirts of Hackensack. Samarkand, built by Tamerlane in the thirteenth century, is destined to look like the Wal-Mart or Taco Bell corner of Anytown, USA. We devour the world, then immediately regret it and become nostalgic for what we've plowed under and paved over. In a shopping-obsessed society that continues to provide for millions a completely meaningless life, juiciness may be the genuine antidote, the real article, a reliable thoroughfare to sanity and wholeness.

Juicy folk tend to be lousy consumers and to hate, above all things, uniformity and predictability. "There is a constant emergent novelty in nature," wrote Henry Thoreau 120 years ago, "that does not lie totally behind us, or we would not be what we are." That emergent novelty, heavy with the heady aroma of God's life, is expressed in us at our juiciest. Jesus said he came to give us life to the full. He meant: Be succulent! Be ripe for the plucking! Be fecund! Many of the saints in the Catholic tradition were your basic juicy people, with haloes post-humously thrust upon them. Teresa of Avila and Francis of Assisi come to mind.

Juicy people are also what author Marsha Sinetar calls "self-actualized." Courage and faithfulness to their inner lights and passions seem to be the virtues the juicy have most in common. Juicy ones take risks. They willingly endure tensions and ambiguities, even big-time anxieties. They carefully assay, but they plunge. They don't treat intimacy like a hand grenade. They trust the wide, wondrous universe is not particularly out to get them, that somehow they will emerge from any ruckus ruffled, scraped up, mangled maybe, but ever clear-eyed, whole. They somehow know the sacred is squarely smack-dab in the ordinary and that to pray is to open your whole self to sky, to earth, to sun, to moon, to the one whole voice that is you.

And we'll know we have arrived at that human, holy juiciness when we hear our kids entreating us to pleeee . . . eeease go to bed.

The Prospect Pie Shop

Miracle-challenged, I guess you could call me. A devout nonbeliever in the tooth fairy, winning the lottery, ouija boards, *A Course in Miracles*, Medjugorge or Shirley MacLaine, personally I have never beheld a vision, seen a statue weep, been dealt a royal flush, witnessed a UFO or even a spoon-bending. As a Catholic kid I heard (and didn't buy) the Fatima tales that included the sun spinning in the sky overhead like the ultimate Texas baton twirl. To me the whole story seemed to say more about human sociology than about theology.

The Fatima story, for example, may validate your faith-ticket with a hefty punch, but at heart shows the spirituality of a bully or terrorist. The Source of Life spun the sun like a top to confound some two-bit communists, but refuses to nudge nature's laws a millimeter when an innocent child is limb-amputated by random Serb shrapnel or beaten to a raw bloody death by Rwandan thugs? Given a choice, in which scenario would you root for some divine rule-breaking? And what do such attributed behaviors say about God?

Ultimately it comes down to a choice, with no ironclad guarantees, between two worlds: one where the God-dazzled sun somersaults overhead, the other where the equally God-dazzled Earth revolves steadily underfoot. Both realms contain marvels, epiphanies and mysteries. I like the second world better (the one where we gyre around the sun rather than vice versa) — less hoopla, less centered on us humans, more drudgery, ambiguity and doubt, but in the end more honest, with a better chance at the grassroots to be a gawking eyewitness at a bona fide miracle.

As a hospice volunteer, my very first patient was a western Kansas farmer who was dying from stomach cancer. His name was Tony. Winter afternoons I'd cross the windswept flatlands along the Smoky Hill River out to his frame bungalow surrounded by crow-infested wheat fields and would sit with him while his wife shopped and his sons did the chores. His face sunburnt and wind-creased, Tony was German, tough and more stoic than a tenpenny nail, with a life behind him full of backbreaking work, never-ending duty and few breaks. Cancer-ravaged to a skeleton and confined to a square cheerless room decorated only by a dime-store print and a plain crucifix, his last chore, it seemed, was to find a soft place inside from which to shuffle off his mortal coil, to locate some bouquets among the rusty barbed wire tangle of his life, a few feathers of grace lying in the flinty prairie soil.

A few days before he died, I sat bedside, regarding his wasted frame wrapped in blankets. Eyes shut, he was remote, withdrawn and preoccupied, with just a flicker of life's current left in him. His skin was yellow and more taut across his bones than his wife's bedsheets. After a long while Tony's emaciated bony hand crept from beneath the quilt, searched for mine, grasped it tightly and held on. His hand felt like warm parchment. My throat lumped in a choke-hold, I have rarely been so deeply touched. The day before he had wept the afternoon away wrestling mightily with personal demons. That evening Tony's voice was frail and trembling, not just from cancer but from grief and gratitude, as he told his wife of forty years over and over again how much he loved her, even calling her by a fond nickname she hadn't heard since their courtship days.

Miracle enough for me, folks! For my money, love and mercy and forgiveness (not to mention fresh sweet corn or the laughter of little kids) are more excellent than a loop-the-loop sun or a hotline to Atlantis any day. A foursquare, fundamental Christian proposition is that the journey to God is a trek *into* reality. Why else would God come as a dirt-poor Jewish woodbutcher instead of Napoleon? We must find God in the world *as it comes to us*, and it's often a down and dirty, take no prisoners kind of place. In any given room occupied by ten of the likes of you or me, there's enough calamity and grief to fill that same room brimful to the ceiling rafters with salty tears. Even so, true miracles happen right under our noses and are ignored. Again, it comes down to a collective decision we have somehow made. Miracles happen far away, not in our backyard. The sun only spins to support some ideological point or dogma.

You see the effects of this decision at work most clearly watching "the news." If I want to learn what life is like, for instance, in poor black neighborhoods here, I can tune in the local "news." The picture is one of mostly crime and drugs. Yet I submit that for every one murder or crack exchange that occurs, a hundred miracles take place as well, as good men and women struggle against the steepest odds to care for one another, raise their kids, even dress up on Saturday night and proudly celebrate their living.

Like snakes before the charmers, we are mesmerized these days by doom and demise. So we miss out on a lot. An alternative newspaper in my town recently ran a story about Rena, an elderly black woman who opened a storefront shop on Prospect, a blighted thoroughfare, where she could sell her handcrafted pies. Her store created some jobs — outside of those in the fast food chains — for neighborhood youths, raised funds to restore the community church and made available to mere mortals deserts that were more like the Platonic template for pies, with meringue to die for. Lots of people felt new hope and gained a little weight. The main media in town completely missed the big scoop. The sun was spinning inside Rena's Prospect Pie Shop.

Drinkin' That Free Bubble-Up

A city-dweller most of my life, I moved to the country some years back and expected to live blissfully inside a calendar photo. Instead this spell wrenched my head clear off my shoulders, for I had picked a valley in the remote Ozark hill country of Missouri. Like the stout Stihl chain saws everyone uses there to cut firewood, the Ozarks can be sharp-edged, treacherous, teeth-rattling country. If you have discovered your inner child, the Ozarks will quickly give it something to cry about. Hard work would quickly bang up your knuckles, beat your ass, then throw out your back to boot. Yet it was also a land where night's deepening shadows harbored rising mists, the calling owls, the star-enchanted skies. The Ozarks could drain off a quart of your blood and smash your elbows to a skinned-up pulp, then just as quickly break your heart with the sight of a bluebird preening its celestial feathers on a cobwebby postoak branch.

When newcomers arrived, old-timers would mutter, "Give them a summer." You'd run the gauntlet of ticks, chiggers, oppressive heat, drought, dry rot and heart-squeezing, gut-liquefying panic, then when you collapsed, breathless, demoralized, out the other side, they'd stack up your arms with spare quarts of pickles, pints of homemade black-berry jelly and zucchini. The people who eke out a living there are as high-spirited, tough, eccentric, beautiful, trouble-cursed and blessed as the land itself. They are hardworking, generous people with hardscrabble lives, trying to stay ahead of bills, but mostly with generous margins around their living, ample time for that growth in their loves and quirks that make us humans mostly so interesting, so worthy of respect.

In our religious traditions, we have only been allowed to imagine holiness in certain ways. It stunts us, diminishes us greatly. This poverty in our religious sense has me thinking particularly of my friends J.J. and SuAnne. Just out of high school, J.J. dodged all but one of the AK-47 rounds aimed his way in the Mekong Delta, then limped home to find his West Virginia family farm fouled and incapacitated by industrial pollution.

He bought some cheap Ozark land and married a local woman, SuAnne. They raised five kids, all blondes with sparkly eyes. She was shy, small, hidden, yet sported the most radiant smile. He was rangy and quietly strong. Life was a struggle; both were up to it — and more. He built a house for them, perched it on a glade overlooking Fox Creek, with gables and turrets in the roof, showing off a bit how fine a carpenter he was. She quilted, knitted and homeschooled her brood, even took in neighbors' kids during bad spells. I last visited them one bitter February night, when outside the cloud-hung moon, as thin as a bit fingernail, peeked down on frosted rockstumps lifting from withered grass. Inside, the five kids were up in the loft, the older reading to the younger ones. J.J. stoked the woodstove to a roar and brought out some home brew. The love in that house shone like the sun. Later that night, I prayed that prayer, the one that asks not for a new heaven or a new earth, but for a quiet heart and a clear eye to see once again that everything we need is right here, right now.

One day crossing the road for the mail, SuAnne was run down by a drunken teenager. Shortly after hearing the news, I was frying chicken wings. As I stood over the sizzling pan, failing to get my mind around her shy smile and quiet beauty obliterated in an instant by a spoiled, overdosed on Metallica fool, and thinking of other such huge injustices (two or three just in our neighborhood recently), a tear dropped into the hot oil, then another, and another. Soon I was outside hurling the whole steaming cauldron into the backyard, then stomping around the block muttering disjointed phrases heavenward: "Things you let happen to people shouldn't happen to a dog . . . ." "Pretty piss-poor Supreme Being, if you ask me. Why not take a politician or a CEO instead?" "Whole damned sorry shootin' match of a world not worth the sorrow and pit of one innocent, abruptly motherless child, let alone five, let alone thousands upon thousands everywhere, every day. . . ." "Take your friggin' free will and shove it!" "Oh, why? Oh Goddddd, WHYYYYYYY?"

We've all been there, haven't we? My "blasphemous" monologue spent, it was back home past the scorched grass and ruined dinner. Eventually I mended my shaky peace with God, but could not, and cannot, make any truce with the notion that somehow J.J. and SuAnne's lives weren't as blessed, holy and important in the cosmic scheme as any silk-robed prelate's, or even Mother Teresa's or the Dalai Lama's. Father Ed Hays said: "The challenge of the saints of the twenty-first century is to begin to comprehend the sacred in the ten thousand things of our world." And Thomas Berry wrote: "Every being has its own interior, its self, its mystery, its numinous aspect. To deprive any being of this sacred quality is to disrupt the larger order of the universe. Reverence will be total or it will not be at all."

We disrupt the larger order of the universe by our narrow religious vision. Well, why would God come as a dirt-poor Jewish woodcarver rather than Alexander the Great? To pray with us that simple prayer of solidarity, and to remind us that, in the words of the great Oklahoma mystic, Merle Haggard: "We're all drinkin' that free Bubble-Up and eatin' that rainbow stew." Every one of us, everything that lives, is holy.

Happy To Lie Down

My sister turned forty a couple of years back. As I dragged my fifty-year-old carcass out in time to get a card in the mail, the shopping reminded me of the disdain of aging that lives and seethes in our culture. Card after card on the racks heaped a joking kind of contempt on the very natural process of aging past forty, of maturing. We heap hurtful nicknames and soul-wearying euphemisms on the aging: geezers, hags, senior citizens in their sunset years. Qualities that come with aging — wisdom, for example — count for little. The end of the aging process, death itself, is a hidden secret, much feared. Modern dying takes place in the modern hospital where it can be hidden, even packaged. We can now deny not only the power of death but of nature itself. We want so much to forget that she, after all, bats last.

Long ago I became a fan of those exquisite oriental landscape paintings, usually done on long scrolls, that feature delicately rendered mountain or forest scenes, complete with clouds, tigers prowling in bamboo forests and monkeys cavorting in the trees. One obvious feature of these paintings is that human figures are almost always included in the misty cloud-wrapped vistas. On the wall of my little study at home hangs a cheap reproduction I found in a thrift shop. In it, small figures trudge across a rope bridge suspended over a dramatic cataract in mountainous terrain. Their mischievous eyes glitter. Always in among the flora and fauna, there is . . . us humans, just folks, women and men doing things. Even in our modern steel and glass towers — if we but pull our perspective back far enough — we are, for better or worse, figures in the landscape, albeit powerful figures nowadays.

My life and yours, in all their details, are as much a part of the wide universe as any tawny-flanked valley or wave-lapped seashore in the great outdoors. We are part and parcel of the earth's existence. Our sphere is within her sphere. We may be more cultivated than a wheat field, more domesticated than a cat, but we flow with seawater, ebb and fall like the tides. Our lives twist, turn and meander like rivers, rife with undertows and currents, nourished by side channels. Slamming car doors, losing our keys, graduating from high school, stirring the oatmeal, these events really are as natural as any great blue heron winging up to its rookery, any rainsquall over the Patagonian plains or any meteor streaking across the black enamel of the night. There are parts of us as uncanny, as dangerous and unknown as any wilderness. There are both desert wastes and lush gardens in our hearts. Like it or not, we are connected with everything else.

For most of us, it's okay that we're kin to the sparrows on the windowsill. It's the fact that we're similarly biodegradable that seems to bother us to no end. What has happened to us? What's going on? Are we so poorly connected with our inner depths and alienated from our living to such an extent that now we are reluctant even to grow old? When we see our lives and experiences as so bereft of connection with the sacred, then it follows that our aging and dying will seem unreliable and God-forsaken. Henry Thoreau once wrote: "I will be happy to lie down in the ground for eternity, because I have so thoroughly loved that same earth in my life." Thoreau had not neglected those inner connections with the sacred, his spirituality.

Acceptance of aging, to me, seems like an acid test of our spiritualities. Do we trust that the cosmos we come from is ultimately benign, that God really is love, and maybe even has wonderful surprises up her sleeves? One of Jesus' main messages in the Gospels was: "Do not be afraid! I am with you always!" Do we really believe that?

At a retreat a few years back I met Gordon from Winnipeg. Retired from ministry and in his mid seventies, Gordon and his wife were busy pursuing a lifelong love affair with the Canadian arctic. The previous year they had booked passage on a supply steamer on its monthly trip from Newfoundland up to Baffin Island in the far remote north. As their vessel dodged icebergs and raced whales, they stood on the deck in the midnight sun and watched the northern lights dazzle-shimmer the vault of night.

Recently we had a retirement ritual for our friend Marie. We drummed, sang and danced as Marie pledged her dreams for this last adventure in her life, her retirement years. Ritually she dedicated her remaining years to three of her lifelong dreams: First, to reverently and carefully savor her life now that she has more leisure. Second, to make a difference, to help change the world for the better. She'll do this by continuing her volunteer work — she's treasurer for a women's spirituality group and for a community-supported agriculture project. Third, she wants to vigorously thumb her nose at (and give hearty Bronx cheers to) our stereotypes of aging, avoiding docility and sweetness, even if it means sometimes wearing a red miniskirt and a purple wig.

These folks may be on that downward slope, but I submit that their continuing enchantment with life and commitment to their community puts to deep shame many a cynical, world-weary thirtysomething or Smashing-Pumpkins-addled teenager obsessed with perforating his or her body parts. Better to be over the hill than clueless, out of real touch and afraid of the dark.

True Eucharist:
Spirituality and Work

In 1974, Chicago journalist Studs Terkel published a groundbreaking volume called *Working*. Filled with discussions and interviews with ordinary people about their work, the opening sentence of Terkel's introduction to these fascinating interviews reads like this: "This book, being about work, is by its very nature, about violence — to the spirit as well as the body." The violence Terklel talks about involves ulcers, tirades with coworkers, kicking the dog around at home or just the never-ending grind of small daily humiliations. A memorable few of the interviewees were happy in their work: an Indiana stonemason, a Chicago piano tuner, a bookbinder, a Brooklyn fireman. But the majority spoke of their gnawing feelings of discontent, of being trapped, a sense of meaning-lessness, of facelessness or futility. Reading these interviews one is quickly reminded that work is much more than just the pursuit of daily bread; it is also a search for meaning.

Work is complex. Studs Terkel points out that work is a quest for "recognition as well as cash, for astonishment rather than torpor; in short, for a sort of life rather than a Monday through Friday sort of dying. Perhaps immortality, too, is part of the quest. To be remembered was the wish, spoken and unspoken, of the heroes and heroines of this book." We want somehow through our daily work to make a mark on the world, to change it for the better, or at least leave some evidence that we were in there every day, chipping away at some worthy task.

For most of us, work consumes way more of the day than any

other activity, except maybe for sleeping. And if that weren't bad enough, most people either hate their jobs or at least, as Winston Churchill once pointed out, "go out the door feeling slightly sick every morning." In the past decade the ways in which we work have been transformed utterly from what they were a generation ago. My father kept the same job for over twenty years; my mother worked in the home, maintaining the household and caring for us children. My father's father worked a small farm on the Kansas prairie. These work situations, commonplace once, are now extremely rare. Most of the resources which we need to live are squarely dependent upon our jobs — money for food on the table, health care, provisions for day care of our children and retirement. We need our jobs more than ever, and we spend much of our time either on the job or getting ready for and recovering from our work.

For better or worse, if only because of the amount of time we spend there, our work is one of the key arenas where our spirituality is lived out, enacted and enfleshed. Our work is a principal area where we shape the world in which we want to live. Creativity, enthusiasm about life, acceptance of self and others, living gracefully, perpetually learning from life, giving more than taking, optimism, peacefulness, courage regularly demonstrated: These are the characteristics of a spiritual person that our jobs challenge us to develop and practice. If we are so inclined, the workplace can be a veritable schoolroom for learning such life lessons.

Once I took a year off to build a small house in the country. I would work mornings at a nearby sawmill, off-loading trim and stacking these for sale to the charcoal factory. Instead of cash, I would take my salary in oak and pine lumber, which I used to build the house. Afternoons I would gather rocks for the foundation, work on framing the house, nail down planking or apply shingles to the roof. Looking back, it seems one of the most blessed and productive times in my life. And I have a house to show for all my blood, sweat and tears.

While building the house, I would also spend some afternoons working in the communal garden on the parcel of land I occupied. For a whole month, I did the hard double-digging required to establish an organic garden in raised beds. Once the beds were in place, the task was to haul in the horse and cow manure, the sand and sawdust that would build up the soil. Then it was time to plant: zucchini, tomatoes, peppers, okra, winter squash, kohlrabi, carrots, onions, even peanuts. As I worked I was serenaded by bluebirds in the nearby pasture.

This time was the real beginning of my serious training as a mystic, I am convinced. There was something deeply satisfying about the nearly direct connections between my labors and my eating from the fruits of the organic garden, and staying warm in the winter because of the insulation I'd carefully installed in the walls. I can recall many evenings lying abed, deliciously tired from the day's work, and profoundly satisfied with what I had done that day. The efforts of my muscles and the sweat off my brow had contributed directly to my own needs, my livelihood and the well-being of the small community in which I lived, unmediated by paycheck, social security garnishments, boss or necessity for marketing to others what I had crafted. It was, quite simply, one of the most profoundly satisfying pleasures I have ever experienced.

The garden work was particularly rewarding. As Matthew Fox points out, gardens "teach us interdependence and groundedness and therefore wisdom." The first story in the Bible is about a garden. Christ's resurrection is celebrated in a garden and, in one account, he is disguised as a gardener. Gardens are a rich metaphor for life and renewal and hope. Juliana of Norwich, a medieval mystic, wrote this eight centuries ago:

> Be a gardener. Dig a ditch,
> toil and sweat, and turn the earth upside down
> and seek the deepness and water the plants in time.
> Continue this labor and make sweet floods run
> and noble and abundant fruits to spring.
> Take this food and drink and carry it to God
> as your true worship.

All our work — whether immediately rewarding or difficult drudgery — needs to take on some of this grounded quality. Satisfying work is true eucharist, a genuine thank you for being here on the earth. But turning over the ground of discontent, futility and insecurity in the pursuit of daily bread can also yield an abundant harvest of integrity and meaning. The bottom line: Our work is a most holy enterprise. We need to look with fresh eyes at our daily efforts and see them for what they are: the most sacred endeavors.

The Discontent Megaliths

Not long ago I dreamed this nightmare: Due to a critical shortage of folks to do service jobs, a new technology was sweeping the country. If you hooked the recently deceased up to car battery jumper cables, you could get another few weeks out of them; you just had to jolt them every eight hours. Colleagues and I were on our way back from the city morgue with a couple of revived stiffs twitching in the back seat, anxious in a kind of ghastly way to do our typesetting and mail hauling. When I woke up from *Weekday of the Living Dead*, my skin crawling, I had to go to work.

Work! Oh, mercy, our jobs! Look over your resume — and see highs, lows and all between. By far, my worst was a mercifully brief stint as a file clerk for an insurance company. Let's call it CosmoDemonic Mutual, because that's what it was: hollow-eyed drudgery and soul-squelching tedium punctuated by episodes of cruel heartlessness, especially to the women. If that technology in my dream were real, CosmoD would have jumper-cabled up a vast crew of working stiffs. One of my best jobs was being lightshow operator in a rinkydink dance hall. Our gig was called the Discontent Megalith Magic Show. We squeezed dollops of food coloring into vegetable oil, dropped in a handful of Pepto Bismol, pressed this between big glass clock faces, then projected these colorful, squiggly galaxies and supernova-ing amoebas onto screens behind the band. Yup, got *paid* to do that, making dancing gardens of light. In between, I had many short careers: as store detective, roofer, framing carpenter, police desk sergeant, librarian, stagehand, security guard, lathe operator in a sledgehammer handle factory, cab driver, receptionist in a homeless shelter, reporter on a small newspaper, mail carrier and typist/secretary.

As all of us well know, work has its many ups and downs — dealing with difficult people, striving hard not to *be* a difficult person, negotiating all those reefs, currents and undertows that come with the usually pyramidal territory. In fact, our jobs can be as arduous, harrowing, fraught with hardship and danger, and as challenging and triumphant as any hero's journey described in adventures or classical epics. Sometimes we drop into bed as wrung-out and travel-weary as any Odysseus. In our own right, we have eluded siren voices, dodged the lotus-eaters, tricked the slaver-jawed cyclops, navigated past clashing rocks, entered the cave of winds and threaded arrows through impossible hoops with unbendable bows. Wily as serpents and innocent as doves, we go out the door every morning. As Studs Terkel wrote: "Work is about ulcers as well as accidents, about shouting matches as well as fist fights, about nervous breakdowns as well as kicking the dog around. It is above all about daily humiliations. To survive the day is triumph enough for the walking wounded among the great many of us."

Work is both our joy and our desolation; it can be a blessing or curse, sometimes both at once. Now *everything* we need to live is tied to jobs: groceries, mortgage payment, health insurance, self-esteem, refuge from the dread ravages of idleness. This greatly ups the ante; it makes cowards of the bravest. Lack of work can be economically and spiritually devastating. Too much work can wear us down to a glassy-eyed frazzle. Monday breaks, and the world starts all over. We spend nearly as much time with coworkers as we do with our families. Like sexuality, work is an intricate web of knots, and it is, like sexuality, at dead center in our lives these days. Our workplaces are certainly arenas for our spirituality. We spend one-third of our lives in them, most of us. Any fool can sprout haloes in a retreat house or wilderness hideout. Our spiritual fitness is daily put to the test, even strained to the limit, at work. The bottom line? Our work turf, however cluttered or discombobulated, is holy ground.

Work makes headlines now. Wages decline and insecurity rises, even as corporate profits hit record levels. Concern about the breakdown of families, neighborhoods, cities and farms relates directly and intimately to issues about work. The near future will certainly be a time when these dilemmas are worked out. In the Gospels, when he was confronted with the thorniest social problems of his day, Jesus liked to take the broadest possible point of view in order to break through to solutions. We might try this, too. Take, for example, the connection between our work and the origin and nature of the whole universe. If the universe is seen as a machine, then machine work best mirrors the work of the universe. If, for example, the worker is just a machine, then he or she can be treated as one. But if the world is seen as a living entity, which more and more we are coming to do, then work too needs to be organic. It must spring from an inner seed of mystery and creativity; it must be involved in some kind of growth that is world-healing or community-nurturing. Interconnectedness, not the machine or pyramid, is the key model; no single part is less or more important than another. "Authentic work," wrote St. Thomas Aquinas eight centuries ago, "connects us to the creative habits of the universe."

Do we not get through the weekdays like the cosmos does — working out of a creatively engaged spirituality? Solving deep-seated systemic problems, both in our work and in our communities, must involve looking at creative innovations: workplace democracy, flex time, shorter work weeks, cooperatives, a minimum and maximum wage, simpler living, co-housing, putting monetary value on helping one another and on cleaning up our world, giving parents more time with children. Like the Discontent Megaliths, we can make work more of a garden, less of a nightmare.

Feeling Necessary

In my twenties I was a mail carrier out of a little Bay area post office. Daily before sunup down at Elmwood Branch, crews would order mail for routes. The guys in my corner of that mail room were unforgettable: Booker, Todd, Charles Tuna and Mr. Simpson. From the mean streets of east Oakland's ghetto, these carriers daily bantered back and forth as they worked, using their own colorful, quirky language, with lots of homemade slang. Once learned, one could follow their hilariously elaborate conversations about encounters with the postal higher-ups, night life on East 14th Street, love escapades or hair-raising tales from their Vietnam tours. Eyes were called *deuce of peekers*. Lips were *coffee-coolers*. *Hatrack* was your head. Wedding rings were *handcuffs*. *Jump Street* was the beginning of something hopeful. The local football rivalry between the 49ers and Raiders found expression in comically epic terms, and woe to those who backed the loser come Monday. They nicknamed our aloof, dour supervisors: The Postmaster was *Deadyawn*; in the office cage *Easy Money* handed out keys and registered mail; *Grimpy* was our floor supervisor.

For useful information, everyone went to Mr. Simpson. He could tell you which supervisors were *bumptious* (easily angered), which ones were *full of themselves* and thereby blind and deaf, and which ones would *hear you* (were mostly human). He talked like this: "Grimpy, that phone booth baby, a bear now 'cause the Freeway Freddies (highway patrol) doggin' him in the early bright on the Bayshore (a local highway). Want some he-said-she-said (gossip)? A word to the wise: I got my stuff out the window, beginnin' to feel unnecessary." *Stuff out the window* meant he was looking for other jobs; *feeling unnecessary* was being laid off, a common experience during those recession years.

Those guys were not only the true heart and soul of the place, but without them not much would have been accomplished save the bare minimum of getting mail out badly. When one of the clerks had a psychotic breakdown, Booker expertly calmed him down, said all the right things and talked him into the crisis center while the supervisors ran around in ineffective circles. Todd was union steward, and he also made suggestions that greatly improved the way carriers' office work was done. They knew everyone, and all about our families, our loves and passions. Disgruntlement was sparse, though unhappy mail personnel have become notorious, even entering our slang, where "going postal" equals berserkery.

It has always struck me how different workplaces and organizations look depending on whether one is on "top" looking "down," or seeing from the "bottom up." Often the disparity is as great as what we discovered between blacks' and whites' views in the O.J. Simpson verdict. We once did a day-long discernment process at the post office, facilitated from outside, to improve the ways we worked together. First we workers met for a whole day, then the next day we met with management. Our two perspectives were as alike as Bugs Bunny and his carrot. For one thing, workers agreed that gossip, so disparaged from the top, was essential to the health, vitality and information transfer of the company. Gossip can be caring creativity seething out from under "top down" efforts to control a bubbling cauldron of life, an apt description of many workplaces. Put another way, from the "top," gossip looks like chaos; from the "bottom," a nutrient.

Margaret Wheatley in her popular book, *Leadership and the New Science*, discusses fractal geometry, new mathematics describing the forms nature uses as building blocks. Clouds, river meanders, circulatory systems, cell membranes, galactic spiral arms can all be described fractally. It is impossible, she points out, to answer this simple question: How long is the coastline of Britain? When you start to measure, you encounter ever-increasing detail, with never an end to it. Science now tells us, in fact, that nature and systems in general cannot be described at all in terms of quantities. One can only make statements about *quality*. There is true wholeness *everywhere* that stubbornly resists being broken down into discrete parts, one separated from another.

In short, we are rediscovering that the world is not a machine, that organizations are not contraptions that can be all figured out, oiled and controlled with solutions to problems imposed from the "top" one after another. Within a mechanistic view, of course, questions about workers' effort, motivation, commitment and quality are answered mechanistically. The only way to motivate us is from outside, with perks, picnics, free tickets, motivational posters and videos. Leaders make us work by finding the right benefit, salary or threat. Without these coercions, we're assumed dead in the water; we, like the world, are seen as machine parts, incapable of creating anything from within ourselves. Sound familiar?

But we are rediscovering that the world is alive, that we are alive. So we welcome back our most human qualities: our creativity, our passion and spirit. Machine model gone, things are certainly different. Life processes are fuzzy, redundant and messy. Information is available from all directions. So perhaps the best way to solve problems may be by tinkering together, by distributed discovery. Fear of confrontation, disturbance, disorder is always the bugaboo for the "top." The new science's view on life offers reassurance, pointing out that disturbance is the necessary condition for growth. "Life is attracted to order," says Wheatley, "but it uses messes to get there."

One more reassurance that comes from life: When you are part of something that is essentially whole, it is impossible to feel unnecessary. See you on Jump Street!

The Secret Purpose of Sly Earth:
Spirituality and Sexuality

In the 1950s I went to high school seminary, where I got the full brunt of education in a spirituality that totally separated body from spirit. At one point I remember a sort of sex education class in which the instructor counseled us to refrain, if possible, from holding ourselves when we urinated, this being yet one more occasion for temptation. In the residence hall, the door locks on our rooms were encumbered with rubber straps so that the doors would not close entirely. The public examination of conscience before receiving the sacrament of penance was heavily weighted in favor of transgressions against the sixth commandment. The message: Do not trust your body. Females especially are suspect, even if they're necessary. In the hot-air balloon of spiritual "ascending" you need your genitalia like you need 500 pounds of lead.

Discerning that my vocation was not to the priesthood, I went on to "secular" colleges. My education was interrupted by a brief military career. Dating and relationships were a large part of my young life, in school and as an Air Force enlisted man. The very first time I fell into infatuation was with a coworker in a part-time college job. She had grown up in Montreal, spoke fluent French, knew how to wear good perfume, read Salinger, listened to Moose Allison and Miles Davis records and drove a jaunty British sports car. One winter night at a party, made bold by some schnapps and zinfandel, we snuggled, touched, groped, kissed — and I remember being completely ensorcelled, enchanted. My head swam with the smell of her, the swell of her breasts, the taste of wine on her breath, the soft, warm texture and yield of her skin. In one fell swoop, we had entered territory I had been warned about in those high school sessions. I remember going home that evening feeling as though I were walking on air.

"Is not the secret purpose of this sly earth," asked poet Ranier Maria Rilke, "in urging a pair of lovers, just to make everything leap in ecstasy with them?" It was so intoxicatingly heady because, like young ones from time immemorial, I had discovered something deep and mysterious. I had fallen in love with the beauty and otherness of her, and also by extension with the rich panoply of delicious acts which constitute part of our living — with life's sweetest, most slyly elegant promises and possibilities. Not only had I glimpsed great mysteries, some deep need of my soul was involved here as well. Sexuality is a prime location where we directly experience our interconnectedness. We hunger for those connections, for physical intimacy, for moments when soul touches soul.

Moreover, we want now and then to feel the blood coursing through our veins, to be magnificently alive. We seek adventure. We want challenges wherein we use our talents and wiles to accomplish some tricky, difficult task. And sexual connection can be such a rich experience when every synapse of our nervous system is engaged along with the best of our imagination, our empathy, our wit, our street smarts and creativity. Sexuality is a location where many different energies and issues meet up.

Timely questions about sexuality: How did pregnant and poor teenage girls become the symbol for all that is immoral in America (rather than, say, overpaid CEOs, old-growth forests fallen to timber companies, or an obscenely excessive nuclear arsenal)? Why do so many people loathe their bodies? Why has loving touch become so scarce? Why do we almost never hear honest, forthright discussion of our sexuality the way most of us experience it, despite high porno video rental rates, constant titillation in advertising bombardments and endless talk show sex conversations? Sex is big business, a surefire way to rile up voters and a source of endless speculation and anxiety, but how often do we really forthrightly and honestly look at it?

Recently in my city an alternative newspaper did a feature article on an innovative program that had been introduced to deal with men arrested for soliciting prostitutes. Ongoing group sessions were part of the mandatory sentencing. In initial sessions, the men were extremely belligerent and resentful toward this program. Yet, at the completion of the eight sessions, nearly every one of them expressed a special gratitude for the opportunity, for the first time in their lives, to discuss their sexuality in an honest and open way. One fellow even signed up to repeat the course!

"If we reclaim sex and touch from the world of commercialism and exploitation, shame and denial," writes Sarah van Gelder, "we may open the doorway to enchantment." And to a sexuality that is sustainable, responsible and wise.

Our sexuality is a special form of communication. Our sexuality is our interconnectedness incarnate. Our sexuality is about the re-enchantment of our lives. Our sexuality is about embracing the mystery of existence. I suspect, too, that the capacity to fully and comfortably inhabit our bodies is closely associated with our ability to experience connection with the body of planet Earth. To the extent we are uncomfortable with our bodies and see our body as an enemy, to that same extent we plunder and rape the beautiful planet which is both the source of our existence and constant reminder of our mortality.

The real sexual revolution has yet to happen. This revolution will involve the discovery of the sacredness of our sexuality. Sexuality is most holy. Let the hosannas ring out!

My Storybook Lover

An ardent science-fiction fan, the Friday nights of my young years were spent down front row center at local movie houses watching flicks with dreadful titles, like *I Married a Monster from Outer Space*. An episode in that 1950s movie thumped me like a ton of rocks, then lodged in my memory. The heroine's spouse was, of course, a disguised visitor from far out there beyond our skies. At one point his human facade slips for just a moment, and his real appearance is glimpsed. This scene resonated with something in my own life.

One day in sixth grade I looked up from my Big Chief tablet. Scales having fallen from my vision, I beheld how good for the eyes Rita Bunting looked with her inky raven tresses nestled on the collar of her blue Catholic school blouse. A suspicion dawned, then grew, that half the human race was...well, not like me. As a youngster in Midwestern backwaters, the unknown, unutterable otherness of most girls around me was my sole prospect for meeting up with sly, unfathomable Mystery. An early connoisseur, the feminine seemed exotic to me, entrancing and beguiling. Girls were like Chinese banjoes, copper gongs, seaside tidepools, flickers from the aurora borealis, a hint of arcane knowledge, even a chip off the block of God's burning eyebrows — all wrapped up in a pigtailed distillation of the inexpressible. An Alien Beauty was manifested in freckles, longlashed eyes, hair that flipped up on end and souls that seemed kissed awake by a Spirit not only most holy but frisky and frolicsome as well.

Puberty raised the ante big-time. Deep within the morose shanty-town of my gangly teenage bulk, hormones kicked in. Then it was off on Mr. Toad's wild ride! Closer tremulous encounters with the Alien Beauty followed; I even fumblingly and in bafflement brushed up against it. But the most astounding revelation of all occurred when I head-over-heels befriended a young woman who lived upstairs from my first apartment in college. Her name was Christina. She stepped right out of my favorite novels, complete with husky voice and black leotards. Her eyes flashed with wit and intelligence. She had an ironic mouth, a wry humor, a stalwart strength, a storming, irreverent mind. If the moon had a sister, Christina was the dark-haired and more stimulating of the twosome. Nonplussed, lost in the razzled-dazzled shock that is prolonged American male adolescence, I wouldn't have been surprised if she had suddenly unfolded filmy butterfly wings and fluttered up off into the evening. I wanted nothing less than to gather her silver music, her darkness into my hands and take tentative sips.

One summer evening when it was too hot indoors we sat, Christina and I, in a back alleyway under a buzzing neon billboard and talked, just talked, until past midnight . . . about things we discovered we both happened to treasure (Tolkien's *Lord of the Rings,* Laurel and Hardy in *Way Out West*), about outrageous thoughts, madcap schemes. That Christina liked what I liked and thought funny what I chuckled at — moreover that she even fancied, just like me, crunchy peanut butter spread over toast — these were magnificent discoveries. I had rubbed a wonderful old lamp. It bequeathed to me a great secret: Not only did I share the same planet with these mysterious creatures, with this Alien Beauty, but in important ways we were distant kith and kin. For me, Christina was a Copernican revolution.

Later in my young life, of course, I fell in love a few times — once during a stint in the Air Force with a master sergeant's daughter. Not only did she have waist-length silky red hair, the most lovely sullen mouth, but she also relished the same music I did (the Beatles, Eric Clapton, Jimi Hendrix). She confessed to me once, walking home from the movies past a newsstand whose headlines shouted of an Arab-Israeli war, how afraid she was that the Cold War would soon warp up underneath us and blossom into nuclear fire, how she was unable to imagine herself flourishing as a mature adult. The same nightmare spooked me. The goosebump sharing of these buried sweaty fears was the deepest, most poignant intimacy.

Passing years hauled adulthood up on the rope, along with its work, its sorrows, trials and quiet blessings. The arduous — but wholly rewarding — commitment of marriage yielded up its own tremendous secret (ta-dum!): that the Alien Beauty I so long cherished in others, the Beauty that lives, breathes and romps in my wife, also salutes a Beauty I have come to discover within myself, and (oh, wonder of wonders!)

find, thanks to participation in a men's group, within many other men.

"My storybook lover," the chorus sings in one of Paul Simon's wonderful songs, *"You have underestimated my powers, as you shortly will discover."* Too much of my religious upbringing planted the notion in me that women were suspect, bereft of the right stuff it took for the trek to spiritual perfection. In fact, it was implied that their charms and allure were distractions, if not impediments, on the arduous road to holiness. That teaching could not have been more dead wrong. For my own spirituality, I would say that friendships with the women in my life, love affairs and marriage have provided me not only with key growth-producing challenges and breakthroughs, but also with the very richest ore, traces of the mother-lode itself. In denying that the Beauty exists and flourishes in women, my early religious education also denied its presence in me as well. I am thankful I somehow got this whole mess wrong-way round. Many of us have done the same.

Among the disruptions of our times, the strife between women and men daily takes heavy casualties: families torn asunder, broken hearts, a wasteful drain of vitality and energy, seething and disruptive grudge-holding on both sides. It's hard to see how this rift will mend. But perhaps the seeds of healing and renewal have been sown down in hidden cracks and crevices and germinate even now. Women are acknowledging their own worth and finding their power and strength. Men are discovering the much-neglected gentleness and beauty within themselves. The "sensitive" male of the '90s has even become something of an object of derision, trivialized like most everything else in our culture. But such males will abide — or nothing will.

Author Marya Mannes writes: "We need each others' qualities if we are ever to understand each other in love and life .... When women can cherish the vulnerability of men as much as men can exult in the strength of women, a new breed could lift a ruinous yoke from both. We all could breathe free." When the thin facade of our differences slips, just like in that grade-B *Outer Space* movie, underneath there appears to be the closest family resemblance, fresh with wondrous beauty, flushed with God's soft-spoken glory. No science-fiction here, I suspect it's fact, that it's our only hope.

La Vie en Rose

Rita Bunting was my girlfriend in the eighth grade. One late summer evening — the same year that Sputnik flew — the vision of Rita kneeling in the pew before me at novena shines bright in my memory. Light, strained soft through stained glass, burnished gold highlights in her raven hair tied with a crimson ribbon. As the choir sang *Tantum Ergo,* then *Regina Coeli*, I remember deeply drinking in the tawny skin of her legs, the curve of her calves, along with the heady incense in the reverent hush of the pews. So mysteriously yet lavishly beautiful seemed both the dark-sparkling eyes of pretty Rita and the shining glint of sun off the golden monstrance, with its pale inner sanctum, held aloft by the priest! I desired to embrace, even drown myself, in *both* mysteries. Clueless how to go about it, right on the brink of life, I left feeling vaguely guilty for lollygagging so much in church. Idle daydreaming, the good St. Joseph nuns warned us, just awakens desires. But oh, Sister, it's like Garrison Keillor said, "My desires were not only awake, they were down waitin' for the damned bus." Those twin desires, represented in dark-eyed Rita and the golden monstrance, were the Pied Pipers that led me on to high school seminary, to '60s San Francisco, to Capuchin novitiate, to both merry chases and tormented agonies, to long solitudes, lots of reading and adventures aplenty, both inner and outer. And thank God for them! They made all the difference!

Have you ever noticed that candles, music, flowers and wine, the stuff of romance, sex, love, are also the stuff of liturgy, our most sacred rites? Yet more evidence that our spirit and flesh are really one. When you ponder deeply on it, of course, it becomes obvious how, as Thomas Moore writes in *The Re-Enchantment of Everyday Life*, "Sex gives enchantment its foundation." If indeed spirit and flesh are one, then this enchantment with the world that lifts and gives zest to our spirituality is solidly rooted in our bodies. It's erotic. Moore urges us to think of sex in much more embracing terms than we usually do. He points to images in the Christian tradition, like St. Augustine's reference to the cross of

Jesus as a marriage bed, that are meant to show that our sexuality has infinite dimensions.

In short, our sexuality is a rich source of religious experience, a great mystery that brings beauty, meaning and divinity to our lives. We, of course, tend to go in the opposite direction, reducing sex to not only just the body, but to the restricting limits of genitalia. In doing this, we breed obsession, addiction and wrong-headed solutions to the life problems this restricted view presents us.

In this light, one of my best sexual experiences ever was a canoe trip on an Ozark river taken with a few friends: It was a day of hot sun on bare back; skin slick with sweat; the cool joy of the swirling water; the smells of mud passing still pools full of salamanders and tadpoles; fragrances of spicebush and cedar on the wooded bluffs and cut hay in nearby fields; the bright songs of warbler, wood thrush and yellow-throat; the hard pull of muscles at the paddle and the sweet Sabbath release of drifting; the spice of sphincter-tightening danger at occasional rapids. We'd round bends to see great blue herons disappearing down the sycamore aisles. Such sights and scents, and the river's warm, caressing breezes aroused yearning, longing feelings. The stoutest blessing was the gritty intimacy with my own body gained through the strain and effort of getting down the river in one piece. We camped on a gravel bar, sweetly tired but feeling like we had warm electric honey in our veins, horny for more such tasty helpings of life. Serenaded by whippoorwills and then a dazzle-sparkle wedge of the Milky Way for company, I fell asleep only to wake in deep midnight to a hush full of expectancy. From far off some coyotes began their wild, keening chorus. Nearby, owls called out. Some kind of secret and awful glory was rising through river-spawned mist. Shaking off sleep, I remember shivering with awe and delicious delight when I realized it was Sister Moon.

Here's Moore describing a similar experience: "I am taken out of time and filled with a pleasure that brings my childhood directly into the present and for a moment erases all concern for current problems and preoccupations. This is enchantment, and it is largely a sexual experience, involving aromas, memories and sensations."

Contact with the real world, its seasons, shapes, textures, smells and tastes is sensual, even sexual. In our increasingly plastic and artificial environment, we're losing this, the secret missed by pornographer, libertine and sex addict, by prude and ascetic alike: *The world is a sex object.* "If we live in this world with a body that we love and honor," Moore continues, "...we may learn that there is a wide spectrum of sexual experience .... We can take our sexual feelings into the world and live a more sensuous, intimate life." Even our workplaces or city commons can be erotic, locations pleasing to the senses where we create beauty and community.

"When you press me to your heart," sang Paris chanteuse Edith Piaf in her most famous number, "I'm in a world apart, a world where roses bloom. Hold me close and hold me fast, the magic spell you cast, this is *la vie en rose*." Hey, who knows more about sex than the French? Since we all *do*, in fact, live on a daily basis in a world where roses bloom, we all — stud muffin and monk, nun and MTV fan, married folk, the single, spinsters, crones, even politicians, CEOs and bishops — live *la vie en rose*. Change your demeanor accordingly and, in your rosy life, fare thee well, *mon vieux!*

Your Big Love-Crumbs

In the deeply religious film from Argentina titled *Man Facing Southeast*, an extraterrestrial being comes to Earth to investigate the disappearance of other agents from his world. It turns out they had all been undone by the unique nature of this good Earth we call home. Agents had become dangerously infatuated with the beauty of human sensory experience. One became unhinged by hearing a clarinet solo. Others were corrupted by sunsets, fragrant perfumes or eating papayas and grapes.

Though a terrestrial myself, I know this problem well. How sense-luscious our world is! As I write this in February, a red cardinal pecks in the snow under the feeder outside, while green beans simmering on the stove, yeasty rolls and a chicken baking in the oven all broadcast intermingling, richly yummy smells. My wife crushes dried basil and oregano leaves from our summer garden for the stew, wafting heady scent-detonations my way. On the stereo, Linda Ronstadt belts out Mexican cantina songs with a lusty, spine-chilling vibrato, counterpoint to exuberant mariachi trumpets.

Do we all not store in our memory album the truly choicest sense-events in our lives? Our very first kiss, meals of new potatoes from the garden served with fresh peas and asparagus, the fresh, biting relief of lemonade on a very hot day, walks in woods fragrant from rains. Once an ice storm passed over the Ozark forest where I lived. A thick coating of hard-glittering ice lacquered every branch and sapling for miles. That night, after the storm passed, we took a walk. A nearly full moon gleamed through clouds that slapdashed across the skies the colors of spiderwebs. The world was utterly transformed into a twinkling dazzle, like a pinata full of stars had broken over the land and broadcast shimmering sparkle. Soft breezes tinkled limb against limb like a hundred thousand wind chimes. Broken pine and cedar boughs scented the air. That walk takes a whole page in my album.

The first gift to Jesus was incense. Builders of Islamic mosques used to put rose water and musk into the mortar, so that the noon sun would heat it and bring out the aromas. In the holy Koran, the heavenly reward for the virtuous features voluptuous *houris* who cater to every whim, create new cravings, then ingenious ways to satisfy them. My own Catholic upbringing was scented with candlewax, wine and incense. Good, healthy religions have always held sacred the senses, both in sacrament and ritual.

Cultures, too, have centered themselves on sensing. The ancient Egyptians were cleverly sybaritic, using lavish quantities of perfume and incense in their religious ceremonies. They invented bubble baths, perfume, herbal pomades, makeup, skin cream, tattooing and beer. In Homer's bronze age, visitors were always offered a bath and aromatic oils. Alexander the Great never left home without scenting his clothes with mint, thyme, cinnamon and almond oil. The ancient Romans bathed in donkey milk and crushed strawberries. In 1492, the native peoples on our shores discovered Columbus, hell-bent after a new route for the spice trade. His fevered quest was a sensory one.

There is a rare medical condition called anosmia, wherein one loses one's sense of smell and taste. One longtime sufferer reported a remission, during which she ate a banana...and cried and cried for days. Sense experts talk about synesthesia, where one sense mode is interpreted in terms of another, commonly experienced when we press on our shut eyelids and see an explosion of razzle-dazzle colors. One person with highly developed synesthesia abilities reported she tasted the complex sensory stew of baked beans whenever she heard the name Francis.

Not surprisingly, artists and writers are high on synesthesia ability. Pierre Renoir and Claude Monet, James Joyce, Vladimir Nabokov and John Updike, poets like Anne Sexton and Denise Levertov honor and celebrate our human senses. Great artists feel at home in the luminous spill of sensation. They doggedly refuse the separation of matter and spirit that so plagues our religious sense. Myself, I love poet e.e. cummings. He writes so lyrically about his love affair with "sweet spontaneous earth," notices overlooked phenomena like "the convulsed orange inch of moon/perching on the silver minute of evening." He once described touching his lover's arm as "stroking the shocking fuzz of your electric fur." He named her eyes "big love-crumbs."

One of our foremost sensory explorers was Helen Keller. Though deaf, mute and blind, her remaining senses were so developed she could put her hand on a radio and enjoy the music. She had a keen nose. "Smell is a potent wizard," she wrote. "Odors, instantaneous and fleeting, cause my heart to dilate joyously or contract with remembered grief." She wrote at length about the piquancies, tangs, zests and textures of our human, sensory world. She reminds us that, though we are prisoners of our senses, we can exult and sing in our chains, that our great love affair with life is also a religious quest. Even mighty Yahweh, in Exodus, asked Moses to please burn the sweetest incense he could find.

In the catechism of our senses, we can taste and see that God is good. Juliana of Norwich wrote: "In our sensuality, God is. For God is never out of the soul." So? Praise our extravagant bodies, our mouths, fingertips, ears, nerves, taste buds! Use your big love-crumbs to savor the color-splashed world! Say thanks for tangerines, birdsong and fragrant spring breezes! Spirit and flesh are one. The Christian season of Lent reminds us it may well be a vale of tears we live in. But those tears are salty, pungent. The vale smells so good, and the sad laments those violins play are oh so achingly sweet. And our Easter joys are double-dosed with explosions of springtime sensual resurrection delight.

Love in the Tummy

In my late teens I hung out evenings in a local drive-in, often flirting with a waitress there. Doris was older than me. I really liked her dry, sarcastic humor, the way her unruly russet hair presided over the rest of her. One night I gave her a ride home; her car had been repossessed. Financially troubled, she was raising her younger sister; her mother was drinking all the time. We talked, puffing on Marlboros, in the dark in front of her house. I tried to make her laugh, succeeded somehow, then she blurted, "You're sweet," and impulsively kissed me good night. I tasted smoke, salty flowers and tears.

Later her unkempt hair and freckles came back much transformed, as the night crevice of a dream will do. "My sweet lamb. My precious bubblehead," she teasingly whispered in my ear. Senses crossed in the night; she looked like the taste of amaretto, this green-eyed, apricot angel. Her hair trailing across my shoulder, I was wiping away her tears. I woke up poleaxed, hollowed out, like you do when you've been visited by a daimon or goddess, but one made so human by the blue waitress uniform with "Doris" stenciled over the pencil-equipped pocket. Her broken life and vulnerability mightily enhanced her allure. Yet there was more here than lust. A key question for my life was announced to me: Is our sexuality in cahoots with the sacred?

Theologian Rosemary Haughton writes:

> We have thought of sex as something which had to be sanctified, brought into the Christian life and made into a means of grace . . . . We must stop thinking this way. We are not asked to sanctify sex or convert it to Christian use. What we have to do is discover the sanctity that is already there, and find out what it tells us about the meaning of Christian living.

One summer night, my wife and I slept outside on the porch. The moonlight fluttered its wan light on the cot. The humid July night air lay like a flannel sheet against our skin. Fireflies drifted through the trees. Linda turned toward me, wiggling her toes, muttering something over and over. "Yummy, yummy" she purred, responding to some dream visitation of her own. "Yummy," she mumbled. Some dam inside gave way, and I was flooded with gut-wrenching love for her, so palpable I could feel it well up and overflow into tears. A checklist of my wife's body, in fact, yields a surprising number of correlations with feelings that are both familiar to me after nearly ten years of marriage and simply variations on the powerful theme of agape. The sight of her slender wrists always elicits the most poignant love for everything humanly mortal; the back of her knees, the downy hair of her neck bring out the most ferocious tenderness. Deeply do I love to watch her brown eyes glitter, flash and sparkle when she's happy with her work.

Our yummy bodies are the real paradise where generosity begins, the true cradle of our love for others. Our bodies are surely the finest handiwork of that warm, moist, salty God, that creative One about whom advocate for the poor, Edwina Gateley, speaks. There's the sensuously heartbreaking beauty of the young: their muscles sliding sleek under lithe, peachy skin — all cool bounce, perfumed with rosy, inexhaustible finesse. Then come the shellacked, cedar thighs smelling of good soap, the freckly sunburned shoulders and flexing tendons of the mature — sure-footed, capable, with torsos thrumming from the inside out. Then the wise laugh wrinkles, the eros-with-brains smiles, the mottled-parchment skin of the grey-haired, as welcome and necessary as autumn's leaves.

The carbon atoms in our bodies are distilled from stars, this we now know. We're not immaculate conceptions but miraculous nonetheless. My favorite Gospel story is the woman bathing Jesus' feet with her tears and wiping them dry with her long hair. It always knocks me out, reminding me of the intimate Christmas connection between sacredness and vulnerable creatures. Mortal flesh aches with beauty and thereby thrums with holiness. The Creator's sly secret quietly purrs inside our cells. Bodies are thoroughly sacramental. "If the soul could have known God without the world," spoke Meister Eckhart, "the world would never have been created."

Marriage is a rich gumbo. It's that combination of separateness and union that is intimacy, filled high with struggles, along with twisted blankets, tedium and compromise, worry debris, crumpled toothpaste tubes, everyday moments strung together like beads on a rosary. My wife writes more letters than she sends; I obsessively clean the basement steps when tense. She is neatness-challenged; I can be tiresomely fussy at home, then quite the opposite at work. Marriage is also two mammal bodies under a roof together, and all the touching and snuggling, even health experts agree, is good for us. Married lovemaking can be like the warm sun or like heat lightning. Especially early on, one feels blessed with enchantments. Loving that includes the heart and mind is always the best, most sustaining, but usually comes only after we have known firsthand and deeply the tears down inside everything alive. Marriage demonstrates our bodies are made for caring; lovemaking can be the niftiest imaginable expression of it.

For St. John of the Cross, sexual intimacy was the effective analogy for understanding intimacy with God (and he wrote the book on dark nights!). "South wind, come," he cried in his *Spiritual Canticle*, "you that waken love.... Our bed is in flower ... built up in peace and crowned with a thousand shields of gold. The spiced wines flow." Yummy!

Not So Strange Bedfellows:
Spirituality and Politics

Vladimir Lenin, leader of the communist revolution in Russia, was once quoted saying that if he had had just ten St. Francises of Assisi in his Bolshevik retinue, he could have taken over the world — and transformed it for the better.

Most folks imagine politics and spirituality in bed together — and shudder. Horrors! Here come the self-righteous with that otherworldly look in their eyes, dispensing guilt and a whitebread Jesus who always looks like he lived too long with his parents. Or, worse maybe, here come the New Agers with their past-life regressions, their hotlines to Atlantean beings with too many vowels in their names, and minds so open that when bent over their brains fall out right past their crystals onto the ground. Or, maybe we see a megalomanic leftist idealogue forcing all and sundry out of the cities to rake potatoes, little red book in hand, shooting eyeglass-wearers in the back of the head for good measure.

Make a list of your own, adding your most dreaded contemporary nightmare. Let's face it, this concept of spirituality comes with loads of controversial baggage. And when it's hooked up with politics, the potential for harm increases exponentially. We are wary, for good reason.

Here's my own personal list of what spirituality is *not*. It seems to me that spirituality is not: **a)** having the exclusive ear of some cosmic CEO or maharishi, **b)** being somehow online with a universal power that is wholly transcendent to the world and that essentially functions like the tooth fairy, **c)** having sole proprietary interest in some treasure map or doctrine that leads to prosperity or the ideal society either here and/or in the hereafter.

Another list, less than comprehensive, of what a healthy spirituality perhaps looks like: **a)** a kind of street-smarts or native intelligence, like musical ability, that enables one to move from a fearful life to a bold and contributive one, **b)** the ability to make connections, to see that all things in the world and all people are linked inseparably and demonstrably together, **c)** living fully and deeply, savoring the pleasures and mysteries of existence, encountering one's life honestly and forthrightly, both its joys and sufferings, and keeping those pleasures and mysteries circulating, **d)** trying to live with integrity, forging an awake and concerned heart down in the smithy of a soul, then doing the often hard and harsh inner work that leads to personal, and ultimately to social, transformation. Such spirituality is universally available.

Spirituality is political. It is about cultivating right relationships — with others, within community and with all creation as well as with God. The divine activity of the Trinity or the life of a loving family provide us with a model. The continual mutual self-gift in love that overflows into the whole universe (or from families out into communities) — that's ignited prophets, saints and sages (moms, dads and kids) — courses through our veins as well.

Ultimately, spirituality is about compassion — literally being-with-others passionately. All the major religious traditions of the world agree on this, no matter how different or lacking in integrity their application or demonstration. Matthew Fox, founder of the University of Creation Spirituality, points out that compassion is mere sentimentality...unless every living being on the planet is honored as sacred, valuable and equal to everyone else — or until we are at least striving strenuously to become so. Compassion is not so much about "doing charity" as it is about making connections. The word literally means "to suffer with." True compassion has less to do with sympathy than it does empathy, trying to understand the experience of others, to see the world through their eyes.

A spirituality that is privatized, concerned solely with myself, my own destiny and my relationship with a deity, is nothing more than a parlor game. Spirituality is about seeking justice, caring for and about each other. It is about healing our planet. Nothing more, nothing less. Spirituality has a wide embrace. When viewed this way, spirituality's climb into bed with politics seems not only natural and inevitable, but profoundly necessary.

Captain Rockwood

The case of Army Captain Lawrence Rockwood received only back page coverage. A counterintelligence officer, Rockwood was among the U.S. forces sent into Haiti in 1994 to, among other things, "stop brutal atrocities" that might accompany the reinstatement of President Aristide. Rockwood is a real hero for our times, I believe.

Upon arrival Captain Rockwood immediately noticed the emphasis on "force protection" even though it was obvious that the physical terrorizing of poor Haitians was the island's main problem. Concerned about the fate of prisoners taken by the ousted regime, Rockwood offered to investigate the situation in his area. His commanders, including the chaplain, turned him down, not wanting to get involved in a "political problem." On September 27, U.S. troops discovered in the town of Les Cayes a prison with thirty Haitians crammed into a small cell. One man had been confined in the same position so long that portions of his skin had rotted off. Rockwood redoubled his efforts to investigate prison conditions in his area, but made no headway against U.S. and U.N. bureaucrats. Fed up with inaction, Rockwood submitted a complaint to the Inspector General, saying he thought the command could be found criminally negligent for failing to carry out President Clinton's directive to stop grave human rights abuses. The I.G. was unresponsive. Finally Rockwood took matters in his own hands. He personally entered the Les Cayes prison and informed the officer in charge that he was going to inspect the prisoners, which he partially did. Four hours later a U.S. major arrived and ordered Rockwood to leave. Rockwood was later charged with "creating a dangerous and unstable incident between the U.S. government and the de facto government of Haiti" and with disobeying orders. In May of the next year Rockwood, a fifteen-year veteran, was found guilty and was sentenced to at least six years in prison.

Rockwood claimed in his defense that he might be more sensitive to human rights concerns than average because as a child his father had shown him former concentration camps in Europe and emphasized to him the role "cynicism and blind obedience to authority played in their creation." Rockwood said one of his heroes was Hugh Thompson, the helicopter pilot who tried to stop the My Lai massacre in 1968 by landing his helicopter between U.S. troops and their Vietnamese victims.

In 1946 Albert Camus wrote, in the terrifying shadow of Hiroshima and the Holocaust, that faith in humanity might henceforth be seen as a form of insanity. He said that if we want a future that is human, just and peaceful, we must daily fight fear and cynicism, and he added that this strategy will not involve constructing some new ideology but "simply pursuing a certain stye of life."

Born the year Camus wrote the above and now past my fiftieth birthday, I survey not only my own life but the history it's spanned. We seem to have dodged nuclear destruction, but certainly the ecological holocaust continues apace. Now, too, the world scene sprouts not only widely recurring Hatfield-McCoy slaughters on nationwide scales, as in Bosnia or Rwanda, but also the rise of a sort of neo-feudalism, whose barons are CEOs of multinationals, their court a slim retinue of stock-holders, whose religion is self-interested consumerism and whose serfs are not just third-world peasants but increasingly the first-world's middle class, us. As Camus foresaw, no ideology, no institution can stop this dehumanizing juggernaut. Some, as in the Oklahoma City bombing in 1995, turn to homespun violence. The only real hope seems to lie in noncooperation, in resistance and alternatives-building. It may come down to just many, many of us with rigor "simply pursuing a style of life."

That life Camus envisioned is actually a kind of gutsy, passionate spirituality involving ongoing conversion, prayer, self-renunciation — an ad hoc strategy for living that is both fluid and grounded, in touch with the Spirit and richly expressive of who we are. It's what Father Tom Berry means, I think, when he says we must "reinvent the human."

Someone said recently that the political divide now is not between right and left, but simply between the hopeful and the despairing. Against the grain of cynicism, we hopefuls craft contributive lives shaped by virtues we hold in high esteem, inspired by the examples of our heroes, folks like Rosa Parks or Captain Rockwood. Brave obedience to authority now must yield to the more difficult heroism of the whistleblower, the faithful vigilant courage of grassroots activists, the passion and fire of the mystic, the supple wisdom of the consensus seeker.

Democracy is vital — even as it becomes more and more threatened. The spiritual exercise of democracy, not just in government, but in our homes, in our workplaces, in our communities, is a linchpin. Democracy has become the ethical core of this "insanity" called faith in humanity, hope for our future. No person or small elite alone has the wisdom now to see us through. No more can some general, pope, star, president, avatar, book or guru singlehandedly save us. The problems are too complex, too immense. Only coming together and respectfully tapping the combined savvy of our God-given diversity, informed by fervent, frequent prayer, will enable good decision-making to get us through. And what we need is not rote prayer, but the kind of searching, sweaty, honest discernment and unsentimental heaven-beseeched questioning we do in a sleepless night, after we've lost our job or lost our dumb numb serenity when the doctor points out grim shadows in our x-rays.

Captain Rockwood's courageous actions obviously place him among the hopeful. He seems smitten as well with a touch of that new millennium brand of insanity — hope.

Hey, Big Shot!

Not long ago an editorial appeared on the front page of the *National Catholic Reporter* titled, "Has Greed of the Rich Eaten Away Democracy in America?" It asked, "Is our nation, home to the super rich and masses of poor, now any different from Mexico, where one ruling party has reigned for generations? Has selfishness by a relative few dashed all reasonable hopes for a better day?" At home the night the editorial appeared I indulged in one of my favorite pastimes, ranting and raving in outrage at recent depredations and evidence of out-of-balance power.

Bless her, my wife often delights in pulling the rug out from under my choicest harangues. Regularly I fume and curse at the despots all around: the overpaid CEOs, the hierarchs, the commissars, the overbearing politicians, the bosses everywhere who don't listen to the ones who do the work, but all too conveniently I forget that autocrat who, having swaggered to his place at the helm, joylessly barks out orders within my own realm. She gently reminds me of this, and I'm grudgingly grateful, because our recurring scenario puts the whole question of democracy and its decline into a more constructive, creative perspective.

In high school civics, Father Vidal well taught us the dynamics and history of democracy, but it seemed an abstract ideal that seldom matched up to anything in our everyday experience. Mostly we deferred to authority; slouched respectfully away from the police; played army and marines at recess; learned stories about highborn kings, princesses and lowly peasants; in church prayed down on our knees, "Lord, I am *not* worthy" and very much regarded ourselves as passive subjects of our government rather than as active participants. When a feisty yearning to stand proudly raised one of us up out of our obedient posture to a stance of competent agency, a glare would wither us back down, followed by the question: "Hey, Big Shot! Who do you think you are?" "No one," was the correct answer. Later, in military bootcamp, the right and colorfully earthy reply was, "Lower than what comes out of a snake's anus, *sir*!" These learnings, habits and self-evaluations make for efficient systems, I suppose, but it's truly poor soil in which to grow democracy, not to mention self-esteem. The slogan for our common dream is after all not *E Pluribus **Efficax**...*but ***Unum*** — not *efficiency*, but *unity*.

Daily I leave home, where I control our money and make most of the major decisions, for my workplace, where a few control our money and most major decisions, then out onto the byways of American life over which preside a small number who control our money and all major decisions. We agonize and/or anesthetize as we see our democracy erode away, big chunk by big chunk. Debating vital issues cedes to slick imagery. Few bother to vote. The two major parties serve the moneyed elite, who get the legislation they want (free trade bills like NAFTA and GATT, a "tough" crime bill) and defeat the rest (equitable health care, campaign finance reform).

The insightful motto, "Think globally, act locally," is appropriate here. What would it take to achieve and sustain better democracy in my own home? To overthrow my fear-rooted tyranny, I could embrace that risky stance found, for example, in the Gospels. An acrobatics-without-a-net kind of giving up some of my tight-fisted control would serve me well, as would a healthy dose of taking myself much less seriously. I'd need that selfless wisdom that listens to and honors as trustworthy, or capable of becoming so, every voice. Above all I would have to believe squarely in my guts that my wife has just as hefty a portion of the spirit of God kicking around in her as do I. For this conversion to come to pass I would need prayer, grace, some bloody sweat and tears, and lots of tough inner work.

What would it take to achieve and sustain some democracy in our workplaces and in our institutions? Much the same toil, no doubt. We would have to trust that each one of us, both by virtue of our participation in common effort and our worthy status as humans, is capable and responsible enough to be included in more of the give-and-take of decision-making or even in sharing more equitably the resources we create. Some of our efficiency perhaps would slip as we did the hard but rewarding work of building a kind of listening, caring and just community between equals, but in the end new, robust life would most likely bloom and flourish. More participative workplaces, studies have shown, are usually more productive.

What about democracy in our nation? Thomas Jefferson urged regular upheavals, housecleanings, decentralization, cultivating vigorous self-reliance. "I know no safe depository of the ultimate powers of society but the people themselves," he once said. Thomas Merton suggested that, like the monastic life, the democratic path is navigated by the disciplines of wise discernment, frequent reconciliation, selfless renunciation and the good yeasting of prayer. Hmm, smells suspiciously like spirituality! Is it possible that achieving justice and democracy in our midst *is* a validly workable spiritual path, maybe the surest, truest one for us Americans?

You and I are America. America lives in us, and our common dream of responsible equality is in crisis, maybe dying. "To be an American," wrote George Santayana, "is of itself a moral condition, an education, and a career." Good news, Big Shot! We are *not* beneath the snake feces, but each a nobly worthy part of a great experiment. Maybe a way to dislodge gridlock, unseat the inordinate influence of the rich and powerful, to once again become able and active participants in our common life is to begin today in our hearts, then our homes, then our offices, towns and cities, passing the buck, this spirituality of democracy. Who knows where it would stop!

Guilty Bystanders

Frequently I entertain this daydream: What if Tom Merton were still alive? What would he be up to? He'd be eighty-one and probably still influential. His enduring appeal owes, I believe, to the convergence in him of three strong rivers: **1)** his willingness to engage in the divisive issues of his day, fusing contemplation with action by joining the civil rights struggle and speaking out with the peace movement, **2)** his rich, complex, imaginative inner life revealed in his books, journals and letters (it was this very richness that led him outward), and **3)** his passion about and commitment to Christianity as a way to heal both self and the world.

A volume of his journals kept during the 1960s, recently released, is titled *Turning Toward the World*. In it Merton wrote: "Christianity should make us more visibly human, passionately concerned with all the good that wants to grow in the world and cannot grow *without our concern*." He felt that any spirituality that does not lead to connection with others, to activities that help heal the world, is just a parlor game, a self-absorbed futility.

With his wide-ranging interests, Merton doubtless would read *Tikkun*, the bimonthly journal that comments on society and spirituality from a Jewish perspective. Hillary Clinton herself has borrowed from its pages. *Tikkun* is a Hebrew word that means "to heal the world." In each issue the editor Michael Lerner calls readers to what he describes as the "politics of meaning." Such a politics is one of heart and spirit; it centers on our needs for loving connection with others, the need to be part of spiritually grounded communities of meaning, the need for strong families, the need to live in a world based on justice and peace, in which each person is recognized as precious and valuable, and the need to have work that uses up our talents and energy for some good purpose. These are as central to a decent life as our need for economic security or individual freedom. Such a compassionate politics is needed at this critical moment when, as Merton says, "the long-term goals of the human race (to establish a society based on love, caring, mutual respect and solidarity) have suddenly become the short-term survival requirements for the planet and the human race." The stakes now couldn't be higher: It's God's kin-dom or nothing.

What we have, of course, is the shortsighted politics of muscle, greed and cynicism. There was a scene in the blockbuster, *Independence Day*, in which the alien invaders zap the Capitol and White House. Audiences all over the country spontaneously cheered this episode. We've had it with government out of touch, with having to choose between candidates both of whom seem totally bought off by corporate money. Increasingly it's oligarchy vs. democracy, the rule of the wealthy against rule of the people. But this sorry state of affairs could not happen without widespread apathy and disconnection on our end. To reverse it all, we will need efforts like campaign finance reform, legislated limits on corporate power, and much more. We will probably need a third party (or more), bodies beyond the left and right that represent the array of disaffected voters and force the other two parties to face problems rather than just proffer personalities who hurl barbs at one another. We will surely need to restore or reinvent those middle level connections between electorate and leaders, a function that was once served by local branches of political parties, trade unions, civic organizations, even churches. We have lost the old framework for political life and need to fashion a whole new one, making democracy a daily reality. This won't come from the top down, but from the bottom up. Even with the amazing new instruments of the information age at our disposal, it won't be easy.

It was Merton who introduced the concept of guilty bystanders, useful in a country like ours that is always in deep conflict over the role religion or spirituality should play in democratic life. Merton liked to challenge his long-faced readers, and he wrote that the contemplative life is a process of "discovering the Holy Spirit in new and unexpected places." Merton was convinced that political decisions are *key events* in the spiritual life, that *taking sides* in crucial and prophetic affairs that are the moral touchstones of our day is the activity wherein prayerful living bears full and effective fruit. In his day these moral touchstones happened to be found in the civil rights struggle, in the Vietnam war and in the nuclear weapons buildup. Now they live, arguably, in the globalization of our economy, in corporate mergers and layoffs, in money control of politics, in racial, class and gender justice, in environmental degradation, in a consistent regard for life from conception to the grave, and in economic democracy.

Tall order to remedy these? Indeed, but here our spiritualities have much to offer. Without a sense of possibility — of hope — without ways to continually renew ourselves, to build and sustain courage, we cannot speak truth to Power, do the difficult work or hang in there for the long haul. *Tikkun*'s politics of meaning is solidly grounded in our spiritual traditions. Recognizing a sacred dimension to existence, it calls us to develop our spiritual sensibilities to counter the cynicism (that voice that says no better world is possible) so widespread in politics. "It is in deep solitude and silence," Merton wrote, "that I find the gentleness with which I can love my brothers and sisters." Wish he were around; right now we need as much of his spirit as we can get.

Show Me

Since I was born in Missouri, you must — as the old saw has it — show me. By tradition we Missourians lust for hard data, tangible evidence. Abstractions make us uneasy. A Missouri farmer, the story goes, once visited his Texas cousin. "Look at my ranch!" the Texan exclaimed, indulging in braggadocio. "We could pack into my pickup before breakfast and not reach the other side 'til way after midnight!" "Yup," commented the Missourian matter-of-factly, "I had a truck like that once."

Freewheeling abstractions fill the air. "Welfare reform" and "family values" are two we hear a lot about. When I hear terms like this bandied about, my Missouri nature looks for nitty-gritty specifics on exactly how we get there from here. Some years ago my wife got the two of us involved in a local homegrown effort that, to me, demonstrates exactly what I mean. The Food Circle is an endeavor by folks in our town to build a sustainable local food system, one where small family farmers in the area can find markets in our city of a million plus, and where city dwellers can find readily available regionally and organically-grown vegetables and meat from humanely-raised animals. We urbanauts need food that is safe, nutritious and tasty. Out beyond the 'burbs, small farmers struggle, lacking reliable markets for their vegetables, eggs and meats.

Here's the larger problem the Food Circle addresses: In 1940 there were over six million American farmers; now there are about a million, with that number expected to show a steep decline in the next census. High-profit enterprises that resemble vast factories replace small farms. Crops grow in regimented rows, sprayed liberally with herbicides and pesticides, fertilized by chemicals. Animals are packed tightly into cubicles for efficient production. Many never experience sunlight or breathe fresh air their whole brief lives. They are shot full of antibiotics to prevent diseases easily spread under such living conditions. Every year uncountable acres of topsoil are wasted through erosion caused by poor farming practices. Public health broadsides warn us of the cancer risks from ingesting too much herbicide/pesticide residue in our commercially produced food.

In the city the problem shows another face. A generation ago we shopped down the street at a locally-owned store where the proprietor probably greeted us by name. Now we buckle up to two tons of rubber-shod steel and shop at a MegaSuperPriceBusterShopper where aisles shelved high with expertly designed cans and boxes stretch off in perspective-boggled rows under fluorescent dazzle. Contact briefly occurs when the checker who passes our bar-coded purchases over electrified mirrors offers that late-twentieth-and-early-twenty-first-century riddle: "Paper or plastic?" Human and Earth connections suffer, and the food just isn't very tasty, adding insult to injury.

What then must we do? Some years ago a number of us gathered in a church basement. We palavered, brainstormed, dreamed and then fashioned the beginnings of a grassroots organization that we hope will bring together small farmers and city consumers. Better markets make it possible for small farms to thrive once again. In the city, we want neighborhood centers where folks can conveniently buy organic, regional produce and meat. Our striving has drawn together a diverse group: the retired, college students, Democrats, Republicans and Libertarians, black and white all working together. Secretaries and janitors serve on commit-tees with doctoral candidates. Co-op supporters and capitalists cowrite press releases. Farmers and yuppies pitch in on fund-raising. We work well together because we share a common dream.

The dream looks like this: Small businesses, such as salsa, pickle and sauce factories, open in the inner city, hiring unemployed young and former welfare recipients to tend the cookers and pack the crates. Our dream features neighborhood canning centers, servicing community and backyard gardens that have become widespread throughout the city. Summer evenings block dwellers come together over steaming vats and jars with the heady smell of stewing tomatoes in the air. Cafes, bakeries and mom-and-pop grocers back in every neighborhood replace the local Fast Belch Emporium, the Get 'n' Go, the crack house or the boarded-up storefront. Vacant lots turn into community vegetable gardens. Kids plant seeds and watch them grow. Neighbors snap green beans and shell peas together. Every neighborhood has a small tavern and a cozy restaurant or two that serves dishes lovingly prepared from fresh in-season vegetables, free-range eggs or meat, with handmade beer from local microbreweries to wash it all down. Most everyone knows everyone else's names. The food tastes good and is safe to eat. Local farmers and city families raise crops with the assurance that they will get a fair price in the nearby markets. The food is fresher. The environment in general and nearby undeveloped land is used productively. Our money makes the rounds within our area rather than off to McFastBuck's corporate coffers.

Impossible idyll or just a tough challenge, at Food Circle meetings you can sink your teeth into "family values" and "welfare reform." Our contract with a corner of America that we know well means small businesses thrive, welfare reform is grounded in real ways and means. Want the poor off the dole? Show us Missourians ways to provide good work to do and a child-supporting income. We feel that we won't get our American civilization back until we get our neighborhoods and farms back, that the struggle will be fought block by block, acre by acre. Solutions will come from the bottom up, not from the top.

Is this spirituality? Sure feels like it to me. I sleep good at night after getting out mailings or helping draft grant proposals. All the proof a Missourian needs that God's at work here, that good work is going on.

The Scent of Green Arugula

Where I live in the Midwest, the red cardinals begin singing by February no matter what the weather. That's when my spring hunger begins. The red birds' hopeful, ringing songs bring it on. Migrant robins return. My yearning cranks up. By March, garden seeds are on display in the hardware store. That really gets me salivating for warmth and greenery. So by April I've planted our backyard garden patch, and by May we get our first Community Supported Agriculture (CSA) delivery. The sight and scent of green everywhere plus a steady diet of salads constructed from fresh romaine, peppery arugula, radishes, sprouts and shallots finally satisfies that spring hunger.

Every spring now for the past four years, we have signed up with a local farmer in a CSA subscription. We pay a fixed amount up front in February or March. In return, we can expect to receive twenty-four or more weeks of fresh organic produce beginning in May and ending in late October or early November. The advantages of CSA are many. We get quality produce first, the freshest pick, the best selection, and it comes before the farmers' markets open on Saturday. We receive an astonishing variety, depending on what is in season. By participating, we support a family farming operation that is ecologically and environmentally sound, locally focused and sustainable. By paying for food in advance, we help keep the farmer from borrowing for seeds and start-up costs. There's a slight risk, if poor weather produces poor harvests, but CSA farmers are usually so diversified that the risk is minimal.

Best of all, we know the people who grow our food. We have shared potlucks with them, visited the farm, perused their organic certification papers. Our farmers are John and Judy Kaiahua of JJ Farms in Raytown, a Kansas City suburb. John is retired from the Marines. His "farm" spreads over his spacious backyard — and over a number of other half-acre backyards leased from neighbors. In this limited space, John and Judy grow enough scrumptious produce to feed forty CSAs and sell at the local organic market.

Why shell out the extra money for organic? We pay because most supermarket food is grown, distributed and managed by a few big corporate giants that in 1995 used two billion pounds of pesticides and

270 billion pounds of artificial fertilizer in agriculture alone. Because the foodstuffs travel long distances and are doctored with artificial colors, waxes and sprays to give the illusion of freshness, it is often two weeks or more from picking by the time the stock clerk neatly piles them in aisle two at the local food emporium. Such wasteful and unsustainable practices not only result in food that is unsafe to eat, but also our topsoil disappears, our air and groundwater are polluted. The nearby state of Kansas came in last of all fifty states two years running now on water quality, caused by agricultural runoff. The anemic tomato that appears on winter produce shelves is most likely grown in Mexico, sprayed with chemicals banned in the U.S. and picked by a worker who is paid $2.50 a day, is given no protection such as gloves, masks or safety instructions and has no access to health care. Organic is not only a contribution to personal and environmental health, it also serves the cause of justice. We vote with our dollars; spending them on organic simply tips the scales back toward a better world.

We like to buy locally as well. As small family farmers, John and Judy belong to an endangered species. Recent statistics show that eighty percent of farms in our state cannot sustain themselves financially by farming alone, mainly because of competition from large agribusiness operations. A native of Hawaii, John likes the fact that he is cultivating the earth naturally. "I plant in half an acre what most people plant in one full acre," he boasts, referring to his technique of staggering double rows of crops crowded so close they are able to create their own shade, preventing sunburn and discouraging weeds. John and Judy take great pride in their produce, which is rich with vitamins and minerals. Their buyers usually get their goods the same day they are picked. "A lot of agribusiness produce has to be picked when it's still green so by the time they transport, it's ripe," John says offhandedly. By contrast, his produce is fresh and mature, which translates into some of the finest eating imaginable.

Not only did we have a freezer full of tomato sauce, spinach, turnips and green beans for the winter, we had fond memories of last year's dining highlights: A simple meal of grilled salmon, along with Swiss chard doctored with plum and hoisin sauce; fresh relish made with beets, carrots, lime juice and sweet onions, with a sliver of habanero pepper thrown in for flavorsome pep. Or green peppers stuffed with brown rice, shitake mushrooms and parmesan. Or ratatouille made with fresh eggplant, zucchini, plum tomatoes and red peppers, seasoned with basil and oregano just picked from the backyard. One weekend we got some lamb from another local farm couple, David Shafer and Alice Dobbs, who raise their animals humanely and graze them on pastures that belonged to their grandparents. We grilled the lamb on sticks with peppers and onions, served a fresh salad alongside and some rice and applesauce made from windfall pippins, green tomatoes and sage, all washed down with handmade beer from a little brewery in the Ozarks. It was the kind of meal in which every bite is savored, lingered over, memorable. Such delicious food is tangible proof that God is good. Lovingly preparing it is a contemplative exercise.

You'll have to excuse me. It's time to send in our order for this year!

Yates Cemetery Road

Call it the Yates Cemetery Road Nightmare. Variations of it often visit my sleep. The Yates Cemetery Road is a winding gravel byway in the heart of the Missouri Ozarks. Following a ridge above Mad Dog Hollow, its surface is punctuated with potholes, interrupted by teeth-jarring corduroy ridges and tire-destroying flinty rocks. In the dream, I'm walking the road as I often did when I lived nearby. I turn a corner and behold earth movers parked on the shoulder, piles of lumber and blocks, the skeleton of condominiums going up and a brand new gleaming quicktrip emporium ready to open doors for business. *O tempora! O mores!* I wake up full of dread and anguish.

Take a walk with me on this remote county road that doesn't even appear on the most detailed map. We pass high glades tilted south toward Arkansas. In April they're carpeted with evening primrose, beardtongue, Indian paintbrush and a dozen other kinds of wildflower. Bluebirds, warblers, indigo buntings and tanagers perch on postoak and redbud branches. Down below in the glooms of the hollow grow maidenhair ferns, watercress, medicinal herbs like ginseng and golden seal, and even rare red and white ladyslipper orchids.

Seldom visited, the deeps of the hollow below the road are strongholds of peace and silence in the winter. Except for the calling of the owls and the faint murmurings of creeks, the nights are silent as the north side of a gravestone. Nothing disturbs the wide calm. The Milky Way grandly divides the night sky, its cascades of worlds making an arched and unthinkably vast banner over the land. Sirius, the star of winter, is perched in pine branches. The Pleiades shimmer directly overhead. Such nights are uninterrupted contemplations that take place before the stripped altars of mystery, as the winter-muted hills ask an unceasingly prayerful question of the star-inflamed heavens: "Who then holds the helm of this world?" Silence is the answer given, and it's eloquently sufficient.

There's human life there as well, of course. At road's end lives the

Nance family, whose ancestors have inhabited this land since just after Andrew Jackson was president. The story is told of how Willard Nance did some horse trading while logging one winter day with his neighbor. They had cut a great white oak, and his partner, Jack, was pinned by the leg under a branch when the tree fell. Before he went to work with a chain saw to free Jack, Willard haggled a better price on the pickup Jack had for sale, one Willard had his heart set on. Part scalawag, part hero, like all of us. Willard's arm is scarred from plucking another neighbor's son out of a burning car.

The critical dilemma of humans and our relationship with nature plays out here as starkly and dramatically as anywhere. The forestry industry, having plundered almost completely the old growth forests in the West, recently moved their pulp mills into the Ozarks, paying landowners tidy sums to come in and cut off all the timber on flinty acres not much good for anything in the way of big cash crops. Though it breaks my heart and haunts my dreams, I can't find it in me to fault Willard for selling his timber along the Yates Cemetery Road. In this the second poorest county in the state, where the average income is still expressed in four figures, rural communities dwindle and diminish, as they do everywhere in the world now. Cities and suburbs suck up their resources, their young, their soil and forests. Our best minds never wonder on what terms a good and conserving life might be lived there. Our best energies seem to be always occupied elsewhere.

By the time all the Yates Cemetery Roads are developed, what will we have become? How will we survive interiorly without such sanctuaries of peace and silence that exist outside of and independent from our own devices? What kind of souls will we humans harbor if we have never strolled in a forest out of sight of pavement or even heard a songbird in the morning? Father Tom Berry points out that our ability to imagine beauty, grace or God depends so much on those varied presences from the natural world that are so artfully devised, so effortlessly beautiful, so graced, so full of divine presence. This is what is meant, I believe, when some, myself included, are heard to say: If our churches have nothing to say on the environment, then they have nothing to say. Our kids' future hinges so heavily on how this issue is settled in the new millennium.

"The question that *must* be addressed," writes Wendell Berry, author and farmer, "is not how to care for the planet but how to care for each of the planet's millions of human and natural neighborhoods, each of its millions of small pieces and parcels of land, each one of which is in some precious way different from all the others." We want to preserve the planet, but somehow this must be worked out at the scale of our competence — that is, in the wish to preserve all of its humble households and neighborhoods.

Only love can do it. Only love can reconcile human needs with the imperative of sustainability, conservation. Not abstract love, but love that is waist deep in reality, in particulars. "The older love becomes (Wendell Berry again), the more clearly it understands its involvement in partiality, imperfection, suffering, and mortality." St. Francis comes to mind here. His twelfth century marriage to poverty and sparing use of the Earth's resources led to deep ecological insight, caring for the poor and the Earth together in the premise that everything is holy. He simply loved creation in all its aspects. Now we need millions on millions of *poverellos* like him. Where is *your* Yates Cemetery Road?

Shake the Dust Off of Your Wings:
Spirituality and Pop Culture

A is for Asimov and his galaxy-spanning sci-fi novels.

B is for the Beatles, and the magical mystery tour of their songs: from "Hello, Good-bye" or "Maxwell's Silver Hammer" to "Lady Madonna" or "Rocky Raccoon."

C is for dark-visaged Captain Nemo, skipper of the Nautilus in Disney's thrilling adventure film, *20,000 Leagues Under the Sea.*

D is for Dracula, the dark side of life constellated in one creepy, sexy figure.

E is for Elvis, who helped hitch black blues up with country music and build a new way of looking at and expressing life named rock 'n' roll.

F is for Fay Wray, who played the young blonde King Kong fell for and kidnapped.

With this litany, I want to sing the praises of our popular culture, that unlikely yet habitual hangout for the Spirit of the Holy. Purposefully I divide the highbrow from the low, in order to spend some time with that portion of our culture that is there primarily to entertain, or to tell sit-on-the-edge-of-your-seat-and-bite-your-knuckles tales of suspense, adventure or intrigue, or to rhapsodize with melodies using popular speech, common sentiments and universal experiences for material.

The best of pop culture is both compost for our imagination and reference material for our inner life. Without it, I believe, life would be much, much harder to navigate and bear.

When I look back on my own biography, I can readily see how energetically and deeply films, songs and other expressions of pop culture have influenced and formed my growth as a person. They have surely helped me find my way through life. Because of pop culture's films, stories and songs, I know myself better: my passions, my enthusiasms, my strengths and weaknesses. The best have been beacons that helped me navigate my way through often ambiguous and confusing situations: coming to terms with and exploring my sexuality, clarifying my politics and identifying my heroes and heroines. Sometimes I wonder what folks did without this wide array of cultural artifacts.

A hundred years ago there were no films, no compact discs, no comic books. People oriented their inner lives by means of literature, through familiarity with Greek mythology, with the Old and New Testaments. Read the journals of Henry David Thoreau, for example, written during the 1840s and 1850s. In the daily journal of this well-educated New Englander are abundant references to Greek mythology and to the works of Shakespeare. Characters from the novels of James Fenimore Cooper, for instance, were as familiar to Thoreau and his contemporaries as Forrest Gump, the Mighty Morphin Power Rangers or Thelma and Louise are to us. Thousands of years ago Greeks and Romans memorized Homer's epics as references in their consciousness. Fictional characters, situations and stories have always been there for the human race. This is nothing new. Only the forms change. While Thoreau had leather volumes sitting on his shelves, we now have plastic cassettes with brightly-colored labels. The result is the same. Stories, characters, melodies and lyrics from popular culture shape us in ways we often overlook.

Assessing personality types, correlating the landscape of a person with a number or a way of perception, is popular nowadays. In the same vein, if you give me a list of, say, your favorite films, I can deduce much about who you are. Make a list of your own beloved movies. Some of my all-time favorites: *To Kill a Mockingbird, 20,000 Leagues Under the Sea, A Hard Day's Night, The Year of Living Dangerously, Walkabout, Night of the Hunter, Breaking Away, Midnight Cowboy, The Wild Bunch, Wild Strawberries, Doctor Strangelove, The Maltese Falcon, Blade Runner, Amarcord, Juliet of the Spirits, Ran, Throne of Blood, The Secret of Roan Inish, The African Queen* and *Strangers in*

Good Company.

That's just a few. I could go on and on. They're like old good friends. Just having known them and spent some time with them has enriched me, drawn forth good from me, widened my perspective on the world around me, put flesh and bones on some of my ideals and aspirations, enhanced my love of life, renewed my optimism, made me laugh and laugh, and supplied images that evoke my deepest feelings and elicit awe and wonder at the mystery of existence.

Some examples will show what I mean. I'll take three films that have been important to my own life.

Stanley Kubrick's classic *2001: A Space Odyssey* (released in 1968). One pivotal scene in this magnificent film: when the apelike hominid, our ancestor from several million years ago, crouches before the mystery of the smooth black monolith, scratches his furry head, then tosses a wild ox's jawbone into the air, which lazily turns over and over before dissolving into a turning space shuttle on its way to the moon. For me, that scene stands as the quintessential image that captures all the awe, wonder and mystery of being human in the midst of the unthinkably vast universe science has discovered and presented to us in my lifetime. I shiver whenever I think about it.

Ingmar Bergman's *The Seventh Seal* (1956). In this great film by the Swedish director famous for his richly imagined investigations of religious questions, there is an absolutely harrowing scene in which a young "witch" is burnt at the stake by a community of terrified peasants during the plague years of the middle ages. I saw the film when I was in college. It completely knocked me off balance, in part forcing me to reevaluate my childhood religious upbringing. For me, this film's imaginative religious questioning forever stalks my consciousness, with its images of stark evil hand in hand with portrayals of good. For better or worse, Bergman's film forever banished an empty-headed or one-sided view of the world in which I live. It's a film that, for me, was a touchstone. It has helped keep my own religious questioning honest. Any deep investigation of the meaning of things has to honestly reckon with the huge and monstrous evil we humans are capable of — with, in fact, the dark side that shadows every shaft of light. Any creed that does not acknowledge this dark side is nothing more than just whistling past the cemetery.

Breaking Away (1979): a film about love, about being young, about growing up in the Midwest, about bicycle racing, about the steadfast love of parents for their children, all served up with the most creative and whimsical humor. It's a rich and complex film whose screenplay — amazingly — was written by an Eastern European immigrant, Steve Tesich. Dave Stohler and his friends have just graduated from high school in the university town of Bloomington, Indiana. He and his friends are called "cutters" by the college kids because their parents work in the limestone quarries outside town. Dave's father helped build the magnificent edifices on campus yet can't afford to send his kids to the university. Dave assumes an alternate identity as an Italian bicycle racer, woos one of the college girls and enters a bicycle race, where the real Italians participate and treat him badly. Dave's parents (played by Barbara Barrie and Paul Dooley) provide a nurturing deep regard, a bemused guidance and support. An all-time favorite, *Breaking Away* lodged in my consciousness, and when I, in turn, became parent for a teenage stepson, it helped me with that difficult and challenging role. Also, this film is a subtle investigation of what is probably the real taboo subject in our society: no, not sex, but class differences.

These films started as conversations in my head that are still going on. Films have power and influence in our lives. So do other forms of pop culture.

What are your favorite pop songs? Popular music at its best celebrates and comments on life in creative ways that lift the soul and inform our awareness. Take, for example, songwriter Paul Simon's blending of South African rhythms and harmonies with sophisticated 1990s urban lyrics in *Graceland*. His particular brand of imaginative synthesis shows me the wonderful new life and creativity that emerges when we honor and recognize human diversity. The late John Lennon helped us imagine a world without war. New Jersey rocker Bruce Springsteen recently released an album titled "The Ghost of Tom Joad," in which he revisits some of the populist fervor of Steinbeck's great novel of the depression and applies it to the factory closings, downsizings and other blue collar travails of the closing decade of the century. In recent years there has been an explosion of interest in the popular music of our diverse ethnic cultures. Music stores are filled with tejano, reggae, ska, kletzmer, rhythm and blues, zydeco, cajun, bluegrass, hiphop, soul, doowop, Celtic, gamelan, aboriginal drumming, and on and on. To me, this wide interest seems like a huge step toward learning to live with one another and to appreciate, even enjoy, our differences.

Pop music among other things has a way of reflecting our experience back to us, validating or assaying it in ways nothing else in our culture does. How we feel about our sexuality, for example, can be explored, and even laughed at, in popular music. Songwriters and lyricists comment upon aspects of our lives that are generally not much discussed or examined elsewhere. Here's an excerpt, for example, from a Grateful Dead song about work. With zestful and wry humor, this song looks at an experience many of us have had as we punched time clocks, working our way toward our dreams.

> Maybe you collect or maybe you pay
> Still got to work that eight hour day.
> Whether you like that job or not
> You'd better keep it on ice.
>
> While you're lining up your long shot
> Which is to say, hey, hey, keep yer day job.
> Don't give it away, keep yer day job, whatever they say
> Keep yer day job, til your night job pays.
>
> Steady boys, starting that eight hour day
> Never underrate that paycheck power.
> By now you know that the face on your dollar
> Got a thumb on its nose and a hand on your collar.
> With a chance to say, hey, hey, keep your day job ....

Here's one of my very favorites, a song called "To Live Is to Fly" by the late Townes Van Zandt.

> Days, up and down they come
> like rain on a congadrum.
> Forget most, remember some,
> but don't turn none away.
> Everything is not enough
> and nothing is too much to bear.
> Where you been is good and gone.
> All you keep is the getting there ....

To live is to fly.
So shake the dust off of your wings
and the sleep out of your eyes.

We all got holes to fill.
Them holes are all that's real.
Some fall on you like a storm.
Sometimes you dig your own.
The choice is yours to make.
Time is yours to take....

To live is to fly.
So shake the dust off of your wings
and the sleep out of your eyes.

Van Zandt's meditative lyrics, sung in his simple way with just an acoustic guitar for backup, is simply a superb anthem to the heights and depths of daily existence in the twentieth century, a hymn for the church of being alive, for participating in the web of life. And our popular culture is full of these treasures, nuggets of gold strewn everywhere you look.

W is for Nero Wolfe, the gourmandizing detective.

X is for Xena, the Warrior Princess.

Y is for Neil Young, falsetto-voiced rocker, founder of the grunge school of music.

Z is for ZZ Topp. And begin again, **A** is for Arhoolie Records, purveyors of down-home music, jukebox to the world. **B** is for Boba Fett....

Scarlet Begonias, Box of Rain

Confession: I'm a Grateful Deadhead, always have been. And more. When I first heard Buddy Holly and Chuck Berry on the radio at age ten, rock 'n' roll, that feisty American music, captured my heart and soul. From the Beatles, the Rolling Stones and Springsteen, through Van Morrison, Neil Young and Joni Mitchell, to Patti Smith, R.E.M., the Cranberries and Me'Shell NdegeOcello, you name 'em — I'm a big fan. We've had lovers quarrels and lukewarm spells, but we've also scaled rapturous heights together and often danced the loose-limbed shimmy shake. This lively music has greatly helped me see the glory, tragedy and creative power that drenches us and our world everywhere you look.

At age twenty-one, for example, in Vietnam-era military police school, with forty others in the hill country of south Texas: We were all exhausted, dirty and dispirited from a long march back from maneuvers. All of a sudden, one of our squad leaders started loudly singing "Monday, Monday," a current hit from the Mamas and the Papas. To a man, we all took up the lyrics. Our drudgery shapeshifted into a make-it-up-as-you-go boogaloo down the gravel road. In a moment, fatigue-clad automatons transformed into a spunky, though badly harmonizing, ragtag of uniquely peppy spirits with a whole new lease on life — many of whom, I'm sure, began to really notice the subtle loveliness of the country around us, or at least the grinning magic this song had wrought in us.

Another time on the West Coast, driving home from a concert in my battered MG convertible, across the Golden Gate Bridge: Below, the siren blast of a freighter bound for Capetown or Singapore duetted with foghorns on the rust-red bridge towers. Past the glittery, bay-reflected lights of Sausalito and Tiburon, I saw ahead the pastel tiers of fog-stalked San Francisco looking ever so bedazzling like the Emerald City of Oz. Off to the right the titanic, heaving mystery of the Pacific brooded in darkness, saying nothing. My mind and heart were swept off their feet and knocked out by how mysteriously and ravishingly beautiful our world can be. The only drugs involved were the salty night air and music pulsing from the radio — the sensual, sawdust charm of Bob Dylan's voice singing with the organ and his own harmonica backup on "Lay, Lady, Lay," one of his best country fantasias. "Oh moment, stay! Thou art so fair!" Thus do we sell our souls again and again to the bright angels of life.

During a bout with serious depression, the head Dead Jerry Garcia's chiming guitar, catchy musical phrases and jugband wailing became sturdy anthems for my slow healing:

> I know the rent is in arrears; the dog's not been fed in years.
> It's even worse than it appears, but it's allright.
> Cow's giving kerosene; kid can't read at seventeen,
> the words he knows are all obscene, but whistle through your
> teeth and spit. It's allright. We'll get by.

His mutinous optimism and homespun romanticism about the real were somehow just what I needed then. Funny, but that's one famous definition of mysticism: a long, loving look at the real! At its best, rock 'n' roll does just that, in an edgy, provocative and passionate way. Best of all, to me, it sings of ordinary life as most of us know it. It celebrates the commonplace ups and downs of people's lives, those who work in the restaurants, office buildings, auto parts stores, or on the farms, navy bases or roofing crews of our world. The music comments upon, notices, pays attention to all those nooks and crannies so often ignored by media and our education or discounted as secular by our religions.

Its best works capture those feelings we all share that make up most of life: that joy peculiar to Saturday night, when you're in fine company with money in your pocket; or the smoldering outrage and hurt when betrayed by someone you love; or those common days when your tire goes flat and your cat has her litter in the clothes hamper where you just dropped your favorite new shirts. It honestly confronts what goes down in the heartbreak workplaces and trouble-plagued love or family relationships in which we spend much of our time. The best music explores all this and raises it to heights of art. Rock often performs those Gospel functions Jesus favored too, like turning the world upside down parable-like so that we can get a better look at the divine within it, identifying the whited sepulchres of our day or rendering the last first and the first last.

The Spirit notoriously flourishes at the margins, where rock music has deep roots. Almost any Grateful Dead song is an amalgam of hard-bitten Mississippi blues, Chicago r&b, soul, old-time bluegrass and classical country. The Grateful Dead were the biggest concert draw of recent times because their music was American in this best sense. There are much better bands, but none whose music was so simply bright and shining and diverse and rich with promise. "Sugar Magnolia," "China Cat Sunflower," "Dire Wolf," "Cats Under the Stars," "Scarlet Begonias," "Box of Rain," "Men Smart, Women Smarter," "Mississippi Halfstep Uptown Toodeloo," "Born Cross-Eyed" — their songs are a raggedly soulful litany in praise of life, Saturday night carousin' and hollerin' from good-time pirates with a keen sense for transcendent beauty.

With grace and pluck we live out our lives in spite of all the heartbreak and devastation it can bring us. For many, that's partly because we can tank up our souls on melodies that ravish and nourish and on bittersweet lyrics that tell us of love and mercy and mischief. They help us keep on truckin'.

Smokestack Lightnin'

One of the benefits of living in Kansas City is the Saturday Night Fish Fry, a music program on local public radio you can hear every Friday and Saturday night from eight til midnight. The host, Chuck Haddix, serves up vintage and current blues, soul, jumping jive, zydeco, funk, doowop, four-handed boogie-woogie piano, Mardi Gras mambos, Gospel, r&b ballads and Cajun stomps, along with notable barbecue recipes and chat about the local music scene and domino games. In our house the Fish Fry is weekend background music, but over the years I notice it's also become, for me, a kind of prayer, though of the "noisy contemplation" variety.

Do these names ring a bell? Pinetop Perkins, Eddie "Cleanhead" Vinson, Muddy Waters, Slim Harpo, Professor Longhair, Gatemouth Brown, Etta James, T-Bone Walker, Ma Rainey, Peetie Wheatstraw? They're stellar lights in the genre known as blues, which is largely the music of black America, what sixty years ago used to be called "race music." It's the seedbed of rock 'n' roll and has become the quintessential music of American working folks. The blues express everyday experience in a mixture of slang, poetry and journalistic matter-of-factness, reporting the daily drudgery, longings, dangers, fevered dreams, yearnings, hardships and fleshly pleasures of urban life. With origins in cotton fields, brothels and tarpaper bucket-of-blood juke joints down South, blues presents the ups and downs of ordinary life and raises them, I think, to the level of the highest art.

And the Fish Fry serves it up every week. One moment you're on the sunny side of every street, as when Beausoleil, a Cajun band, plays "Jolie Blonde." Here is more celebration of the joy in life than in a dozen chorused Odes to Joy put together, as the accordian and fiddle weave under and above the happy-it's-Saturday-night voices. The insistent rhythm makes you not only glad you've got a body, but you can't resist showing that gratitude by getting up and moving around in ways you seldom move when you're, say, at work. Next song on the playlist, you're on the down-and-dirty dark side of life, wallowing in the old *Via Negativa*. When B.B. King sings "The Thrill Is Gone," it's an aching but soaringly lyrical lament for all romantic love that's ever slid off the fulsome edge of delight into disillusion and betrayal. In the words of writer Walter Mosley, "The blues is all about getting so close to pain that it's like a friend, like somebody you love."

It is worth noting that much of this music comes from the underbelly of society, from the oppressed, the marginalized, the folks who do the sweaty work, people who come up short from paycheck to paycheck, with calloused hands and grime down in the creases — in fact, the kind of people Jesus liked to hang with. Plus, add two centuries and more of racism, and you discover all the savvy and creativity needed to not only survive but, at least in the art of living, to flourish. Not to romanticize them, but these ordinary people did the extraordinary. They made guitars wail like banshees, sing like pumped-up linnets, weaving around melodies with chiming arabesques, intricate harmonies or daring dissonances. Their harmonicas became as expressive as symphony orchestras. Bluesmen and women take ordinary life and exalt it to the heights of art. Blues makes poetry out of the slang and grit of everyday speech. Blues finds grace, like great heaped slabs of tangy, tasty barbecue, in the seediest back alleys and most unlikely corners of life.

The Fish Fry has introduced me to giants like the legendary Robert Johnson, with his hands like spiders and his voice a hoarse haunt that journeys out to the knife-edge of human experience. Folks who traveled with Johnson said he could carry on a conversation in a roomful of people while the radio was playing in the background, ostensibly paying no attention to the radio, yet the next day play note for note whatever songs had been on the air.

Then, there's my favorite: Howlin' Wolf. His voice dark with menace, his songs punctuated with spine-chilling falsetto howls and moans, Wolf wove, with almost supernatural ferocity, fever dreams out of the syncopated bounce, the tortured chords and unrelenting bass of the blues. Sam Phillips who "discovered" Wolf (and Elvis Presley as well) said, "He sang with his damn soul, and this is where the soul never dies." Listen to one of his great classics, "Smokestack Lightnin'" and hear an art form torn down to the ground, then built back up again before your very ears. Wolf sounded like the hounds of hell were on his raggedy tail, but his music lifts me with its honest, highly original and artful presentation of life's twists, turns, stabs and pratfalls, its plentiful humor and abundant tragedies.

We need that lift. The Fish Fry reminds me that without music life would truly be much less bearable, even navigable. "You need music." claimed the late Jerry Garcia. "I don't know why; it's probably one of those Joe Campbell questions, why we need ritual. We need magic, and bliss, and power, myth, celebration and religion in our lives, and music is a good way to encapsulate a lot of it."

I remember too that contemplative living doesn't have to always be quiet. Every Saturday night this music helps me see that God is not much like a king or lord. God is more like the grass that pushes up through slabs of concrete, more like the hard, aching but sustaining beauty heard in the lively laments of the poor. God's life in us is more like good music, like jumping jive, like blues.

Da Sensawonda

Anyone who regularly watches *Star Trek: The Next Generation* reruns delights in the portrayal of a future that is wholly integrated along gender, racial, national and the most broadly defined ethnic lines. Differences among life forms are the rich ground of diversity upon which this future society thrives. Surely there's a connection between this egalitarian status quo and the sweeping cosmic vistas on view outside the starship's windows. Accurate knowledge of the heavens and a sense of exactly where we fit into the universe seem to make us act differently, even influence the way our societies are organized. As conditions on the *Enterprise* suggest, cosmology can change us — for the better.

Also enjoyable is the contrast between the humans and the android crew member, Commander Data. Beneath Data's understated charm are awesome powers and abilities. Data computes with lightning speed, is invulnerable and immortal. In a New York minute you would trade in your humanity for just one-tenth of his powers. Many episodes, however, end up showing that we humans in our own ways are truly his equal, even though we cannot heal ourselves instantly or pick up massive objects. Many installments of the series are variations on this one theme: Our intuition that we mortals mean something *means something*. We humans have magnificent abilities in our own right. Some of the grace of the Mystery behind the universe abides in us.

Having praised *Star Trek*, let me say that I'm always disappointed by it as well, by its earnest but unimaginative blandness compared to the real universe we both know and can speculate about. A product of the nearly brain-dead TV industry, *Star Trek* simply falls short of the best science-fiction, a proud genre of literature someone from Brooklyn once labelled as "da Caretaker of da Sensawonda." *Star Trek* pales in the presence of the quirky cautionary tales of Philip K. Dick or the sociological extrapolations of Ursula Le Guin or the grand entertainments of Robert Heinlein. No episode has ever provoked the goosebumpy mind-stretching routinely offered by Isaac Asimov, Larry Niven, Joanna Russ, Brian W. Aldiss or even Stanley Kubrick's movie *2001: A Space Odyssey*. This film was adapted from a story by Arthur C. Clarke, another sci-fi giant. Thus, it lives within a twelve-billion-year-old universe that contains some 100 billion galaxies, each with 100 billion or so stars. The best science-fiction is informed by such majestically unimaginable scope and by the magnificently mysterious beauty that is revealed when we peer up into the night sky.

Like the finest sci-fi craftspeople, Kubrick was wise enough not to try showing advanced extraterrestrial life directly, knowing well that the deepest mysteries can only be adequately described with metaphor. Good science-fiction instinctively knows what to do with da Sensawonda. It hooks the ineffable to analogies as best it can, takes the deepest puzzles, the most prickly apprehensions and the choicest adventures in our minds, then spins spellbinding tales around the campfire that raise our neckhairs and prickle our skin with the most delicious awe and even fear. The best sci-fi wholeheartedly concurs with what scientist Loren Eiseley once wrote: "The universe is as mystical as the Great White Whale."

For a taste, here's a sampling of short-story titles from a recent sci-fi anthology. They read like a litany of praise to da Sensawonda, haikus about the marvelous. Here goes: *They Found the Angry Moon, The Reincarnation of Sweetlips, The Start of the End of It All, A Life of Matter and Death, The Mould-Kissers, Aerial Reconnaissance of a Conflagration of the Heart, The Very Flesh of God Is Compound Eye, The Discontinuum Kitchen, The Scalehunter's Beautiful Daughter, Emerald City Blues, In the Season of the Dressing of the Wells,* and (my favorite) *How Erg the Self-Inducting Slew a Paleface.* A sample reveals this literature's rich texture, its frisky curiosity and full-bodied sense of mystery, hints of fantastic secrets barely glimpsed, a wry humor and adept sensuousness that flat-out enchant and ensorcel our imaginations.

Another Caretaker of da Sensawonda has traditionally been our religion. In bygone ages religion's very livelihood and stock-in-trade was contact with the wholly other, the mysterious, the miraculous. For stories of such meetings, see the Bible, where Moses chats with a burning bush, a cosmic whirlwind stumps old man Job, or playful, creative Wisdom frolics before time began. These are, at least in part, the results of our spiritual ancestors looking around themselves open-eyed and wrestling with their own biggest questions, speculating about the deepest unknowns — kind of like good science-fiction does now.

We have relegated such tales of genuine religious experience to the pedestal of holy writ, at the same time ignoring their contemporary counterparts. Religion has abandoned its age-old role as a Caretaker of Wonder to scientists. Who, now that Carl Sagan is gone, chats with stars? Who pens praiseful psalms after witnessing titanic collisions between comet fragments and Jupiter's soupy maelstrom? A quarter century after our walk on the Moon, we know that whole galaxies, with more stars in them than all the people who have ever lived on Earth, are running away from us at nearly the speed of light or disappearing into enigmatic holes like the Cheshire Cat's smile. Yet who, other than the occasional poet, is astonished with amazement, shaken Job-like to the soul, deep-down touched, wondrously moved?

Our religious expressions are no longer informed by our best understanding of things. There are far too few water holes staked out where da Sensawonda's thirst can be slaked. Those of us who regularly ditch church for the sci-fi shelf at the library or tune in on a good nature documentary or follow Captain Picard and crew, toss and turn some nights with bittersweet aches and yearnings we can't even name, let alone find a homily or sacrament for.

Creation-spirituality gurus Thomas Berry and Brian Swimme urge hooking our spirituality back up to the best cosmology. For even some of the most hardheaded scientists now tell us, computer printouts in hand, that creation is not the inert artifact of a remote, solely transcendent deity, but the very living body or garment of an omnipresent, indwelling Divinity. A playful, creative Wisdom devised electrons wilier than a coyote that gang up in molecular lattices which, with a clever mind of their own, build amethysts, otters, orioles, us, and who-knows-what, all living near comet-haunted suns in galaxies vast and far-flung.

Modern faith bets that intricate majesty and unimaginable scale are meaningful. Since this ultimate meaning guides our living, our very moral sense grows squarely out of our vision of God's solid connections with a dazzling, stunningly magnificent universe. "Such a God," says Anthony Gilles, "deserves *more* than our moral rectitude; that God deserves our wonder and praise, even our *enjoyment*." A God who is capable of such craft and subtlety is one to desire for company. Hell doesn't deter us from sin as well as the heavens allure us away from it!

Future generations may someday judge that one of the greatest sins of our age was that we rendered our churches boring and irrelevant to our everyday lives and to the best quests of our minds. We trivialize even our worship. Our spiritual ancestors had enough sense to duck and hide among rock clefts when the backparts of the Mystery, tremendous and fascinating, passed near. Among other things, God is a live wire, an ornery imaginative story lover, probably a sci-fi fan. Meister Eckhart said, "God is *novissimus*! (the newest thing there is)." Author Annie Dillard confessed that at church sometimes she felt she should be wearing, not a bonnet, but a crash helmet. Praying in such a presence can very often be "to boldly go where no one's gone before."

Drunk in a Midnight Choir:
Spirituality and the Inner Life

Like a bird on a wire, like a drunk in a midnight choir
I have tried, in my way, to be free.
— Leonard Cohen

Scenes from a life, a life with both an outside and an inside. Hands busy, some prayer going on, heart traveling like a restless cable TV viewer changing channels, between wonder and grief, astonishment and dismay, clarity and confusion:

♦ I was fourteen years old, an altar boy: My two hands cradled the leather-bound mass book held before an archbishop intoning the *kyrie* at solemn high mass in the Kansas City cathedral. In a blaze of candlelight amid clouds of incense, the prelate navigated the tricky plainsong notes, while I squelched my squirming from a chigger's itch somewhere under the elastic in my underwear. The yearningly plaintive response of the choir echoed against the lofty ceiling, sending goosebumps across my itching. The tingle and pierce of awe at the soaring beauty of the chorused voices tightened the skin around my skull.

♦ I was twenty-five, a college student: Up in the hills above Oakland, California, these same hands gripped the brass eyepiece of a huge telescope, whose mirrors were up to the task of peeking at the Andromeda galaxy, a neighboring swarm of stars 250 million light years away from our home galaxy. In that galaxy are crowded a hundred billion stars. And in the universe we inhabit, there are a hundred billion galaxies. I scanned the stars in the heavens, which are more numerous than the grains of sand on all Earth's beaches. My prayer then was a gasp, the deepest Wow, a heart-centered buzz, stabs of thrilling excitement below those far-flung and fire-featured heavens.

♦ My father had a stroke in 1982. Good doctors yanked respirator wires, and ten minutes later he was dead. Under bright lights on a chrome table, his limp, unresponsive hand rested in both of mine. Until it was over I mumbled past an aching logjam in my throat Hail Marys and a heartfelt lament, "O my God, I am heartily sorry . . . ," in a sob for my unspoken love, surprised that these boyhood prayers had shown up. Those scraps and shreds, though, kept me from shattering into a million pieces.

♦ These same hands once, way past midnight on a floodlit Minuteman missile silo, circled the lead-shielded tip of what was euphemistically called the reentry vehicle, the business end of this lethal, ballistic thermonuclear warhead. In this summer of 1969 I was a sergeant in the Air Force, assigned as a guard. A targeting crew worked bleary-eyed overtime down in the hole. Topside it was just the warhead, wrapped in nylon webbing, and me. Foresworn from prayer then, all I knew was that sleek and metallic in my grasp was the gear that could make real the Cold War nightmare that slouched into my sleep again, then again, like the dread rough beast it was — our world ending in nuclear fire, us and everyone we love and everyone else blasted into a maelstrom of scorch.

♦ A year later on a back road in Sonoma County, California, under a grove of live oaks, a frenzy took place in the dark of my car with my first serious love. My left hand was tangled in her long red-golden hair. My right, inside her silken blouse and under her bra, slid between the softest smoothnesses. I beseeched whatever busy, worried angels watch over young love, in vain, that she wouldn't stop progress until my urgent ache and sweet hunger were somehow in the girlgrace mystery and perfumed architecture of her transformed into something that made some sense for *both* of us. Yet unaware that love's calamities leak hurts and sorrows every which way like a carafe made of fishnets, in those slaphappy days I volunteered for every testosterone-inspired mission, always full of unspoken questions: What did these astonishingly heady feelings mean? How to deal with them? Why, though they are linked with the most exquisitely delicious and deeply mysterious of moments, am I told they are dirty, degraded, sinful? Why? What? How? Where? When?

♦ Ten years after that my hands were bleeding, scratched and calloused from building a small house in the glimmering charm of the Missouri Ozarks. The house itself was a kind of prayer roughed out in oak, pine and mortar; and it became a center out of which I lived in quiet intimacy with the natural world around me. Wild orchids and papaws bloomed in the nearby hollows. My nearest neighbors were owls, flying squirrels, whippoorwills and big pileated woodpeckers that cackled and shrieked out loud and whacked the pines so solidly with their beaks that the forest would echo with their hammering.

The above experiences, central to my own inner life, capture my life's largest quandaries, its passions, its greatest challenges. I grew up in the second half of the twentieth century, in the old church, matured in the post-Vatican II years and during the Vietnam and the Cold Wars. Most of my life was lived under the shadow of nuclear war, in the midst of huge social and ecclesial ferment and seismic change. Finding ways to heal the great travail of the earth, integrating the mystery of sexuality into my life in an honest and unexploiting way, and finding ways to respond to the justice issues of my day (peace, civil rights, gender equality, the widening disparity between rich and poor) have defined much of my life's striving. My passions and enthusiasms — simple living, the concerns of creation spirituality, the adventuresome dialogue between science and religion, living in community with nature and with others, workplace and grassroots democracy — are my ways of working out responses to the challenges of my life and the world in which I dwell. Just like me, you have such challenges, though they probably differ somewhat from mine. Like me, you have such passions and enthusiasms, and you know what they are.

My life is a dance to a tune played by the pipers who are those challenges and passions. These inner dynamics have led me to living for years in the woods in a small cabin, to working as a hospice volunteer, to devouring every book I could find on the discoveries of science in the twentieth century, to a lifelong love affair with the natural world, to an avid interest in how sexuality is honorably and creatively integrated into life, and to a passionate interest in spirituality, the search for wholeness. You know those places to which your loves have led you. Like me, you can hum shreds of that tune to which you dance.

Any of us can assemble an album, such as I did, of deeply significant and unfathomable moments in our inner lives, those experiences that define and shape us. And we should! I urge you to honor your own living, for your life is a sacred journey.

A Sacred Place: Our Inner Life

Like a missing tooth, there are incidents in a life that memory probes and worries at, then arranges like snapshots keeping each other company in an intimate album. Among key life events are: the very earliest scenes from childhood; love's discoveries, hurrahs and smolderings come to flame; our most eccentric heresies; life's worst bludgeonings; the burning bushes; the very best sunlit hours; our fanciest footwork during the most unwelcome testings. The big mistake is to figure that these scenes, these details do not add up to something very important. These are not just knickknacks, souvenirs from travels dust-gathering on a shelf, or even a gallery of kids' crayon sketches stuck on the fridge door.

These are genuine religious experiences, and they are sacred. They are the building blocks of a robust and full-bodied inner life. Without them we are merely hurried, hapless tourists rushing to catch the next red-eye flight to nowhere, trapped by too much luggage in the endlessly revolving terminal doors of triviality. With them, though, we can build that little house of cards, the holy place and reliquary that rests like the wind inside us. And what do we call that sanctum, that inner tabernacle? Usually by our own name.

I want to explore that holy spot — the deep inside of our own living — and to say a good word about it, to talk it up and call down praiseful alleluias on its behalf. Indiana Jones notwithstanding, it is where the most superlative adventures take place. It is the launch pad for our finest efforts and hours, the cloister where encounters with the deepest mysteries occur, the center out of which our goosebumps emerge, the bull's-eye most surely struck by the arrows of awe. It is where our bliss dwells — and our deepest terrors as well — and it is the wellspring for both our best joys and our saltiest tears.

Significant landmarks and events in our inner life when remembered and arranged in some kind of order represent a kind of holy writ for our own lives. Those who journal know this. If we are awake and alive, then we have our own creation myths, our own salvation story, our own miracles when we multiply the loaves and fishes or turn water into wine, our own descents into hell, our own emptyings, crucifixions, resurrections and transfigurations. This is not to say that we are equivalent to divinity, only that divinity dwells and works within us, deep down in the interior of each human life. We are touched by and touch the sacred in our lives. A key effort in the resurgence of mystical Christianity is the recognition that each one of us needs to cultivate his or her inner life. We need to recognize and honor our own life experiences. Our inner life is the ongoing discovery of God at work within us.

There is a contemporary spiritual malady that Protestant theologian Sallie McFague describes this way: "The most prevalent spiritual disease of our time is not wanting to be here, not wanting to be in a physical body." There is a twofold cure: One part involves becoming comfortable with one's body; the other key part is to befriend one's deepest insides, one's soul. To encounter this great mystery of our existence, that we are embodied spirits, is to partake in a commonplace miracle.

The Call to Be Mystics

Poet Marilyn Sewell reports how her poetry reading was screened out of a church workshop once. The poems she wanted to read were about her mother's death. The workshop coordinator told her she couldn't read these poems in her church. "Why not?" asked Sewell. "They're too . . . *intense,*" was the answer. Sewell reflects, "Truth tends to shake us to our very bones. For God's sake, what *should* the church be about?"

Religion should be about the holiness and mystery of our individual lives. When we listen to, honor and take direction from our own religious experiences, we are well on the way to becoming mystics. The great Catholic theologian Karl Rahner contended that if Christianity cannot recover its mystical dimension as the millennium turns, then it has absolutely nothing to offer. The awakening of interest in spirituality that has occurred over the last several decades includes a hefty portion of interest in mysticism. Mysticism is an ancient tradition in Christianity. And mysticism squarely concerns itself with the experiences we all have of the divine in our lives.

"Every creature," wrote Meister Eckhart, "is a book about God." Divine revelation is found in our religious traditions, in Scripture. God's *primary* revelation, however, is found in nature. If nature reveals God to us, and if our lives are part of nature (as they surely are), then it follows that *we* are volumes of revelation about God. Our lives are unfolding scriptures that reveal the divine at work. Authentic spirituality is intimately related to firsthand experience. It may mature through such disciplines as structured meditation and verbalized prayer, but, one way or the other, it begins in — or must find its way into — our own living.

Many are saying today that we need to retrieve that experiential base of religion. We need to ground our religious searching in personal experience. This is how we find that fire in the belly that keeps us keeping on. This is how we locate real nourishment to offer to our young people, who are also hungry for meaning and significance. Some symptoms of a spirituality that is not grounded in real living, according to Jungian Frederick Franck, are these: sentimentality, proselytizing, fanaticism, holier-than-thou delusions, superstitions, spiritual tourism, self-absorbed solipsism and the idolatry of fundamentalism. The primary symptom is unconcern, detachment from the suffering, injustice and violence constantly being visited on the great majority of our fellow humans, especially the poor.

The Inner Life and the Life of Christ

The "interior" or inner life has always been an important element in Christian spirituality. One classic text, *The Three Ages of the Interior Life*, by Father Reginald Garrigou-Lagrange, OP, lays out in great detail the dynamics and geography of our interior spiritual life. The author presents the interior life as "the one thing necessary" referred to by Jesus when speaking with Martha and Mary. The author defines it as the life of the soul with God, the intimate conversation one has within oneself all through life. He describes the stages of the interior life devised by St. John of the Cross and elaborated upon by Teresa of Avila: the purgative, illuminative and unitive stages.

St. Francis de Sales' *Introduction to the Devout Life*, written in the seventeenth century, was still recommended when I was in high school seminary in the early 1960s, as was Tanqueray's *The Spiritual Life*. St.

Ignatius' *Spiritual Exercises* and *The Imitation of Christ* by Thomas a Kempis were other oft-read classics. Conformity to the life of Christ has always been an essential element in the interior life. There is a long mystical tradition in Christianity which honors personal religious experience and presents a dynamic in which one's own personal experiences are taken to the life of Christ for validation, empowerment and direction.

Part of Trappist monk and writer Thomas Merton's enduring appeal is surely the presentation in his writings of a contemporary human soul struggling with the challenges of his time, yearning to live in God's presence, constantly in touch with the illumination that is the life of Christ. Merton's works are reflective reports of the ongoing progress of a man with a deep and rich inner life. This man who was a hermit, yet still deeply involved in the woes and public policies of his time, takes our hand and invites us to walk along with him on his spiritual journey. As we read his journals and essays, we find ourselves often musing, "Yes, that's how it is with me too," or "Yep, he's right. I need to *do* something about that in my life."

Merton insisted that Christ's life is the touchstone for our own inner lives. Merton reminded us that Jesus never retreated from the social and political problems of his day into a private nirvana. He lived among the poor and marginalized. He was human; he sweated, got sore feet and chapped lips. He laughed loudly, cried bitterly and loved deeply. He spoke truth to Power to such an extent it brought a death sentence down on his head. Above all, he took his direction from his own inner depths. Prayer and solitude were both the mainstays of and the compass for his spiritual life. In the end he surrendered this life back to the source of all life.

Jesus said, "The reign of God is within you" (Luke 17: 21). We live in a time when there is much searching for that divinity at work within. Native American spiritualities, Eastern spiritualities and those elements of our own Christian tradition that can lead us to that indwelling God are immensely popular. Merton is a good model for balance in this approach. His starting point in the spiritual quest was always his own life experience, which he took to his own beloved Catholic tradition for illumination, critique, direction and validation. He stayed within his own tradition but looked to other traditions for enlightenment and insight, becoming greatly interested in, for example, Zen. He had a solid connection with his own Christian spirituality, not in spite of a rich inner life, but *because* of it. "Christianity," he wrote in his journal, "should make us more visibly human, passionately concerned with all the good that wants to grow in the world and that cannot grow *without our concern*."

Merton saw the interior life as primarily the tension between contemplation and action. The inner dynamics that come alive within each one of us and drive our spiritual searching derive from the very nature of God, as we experience that nature. Christian theology holds that God is both immanent and transcendent. This means that God as immanent is directly and personally present in our own being, at work within us every day of our lives. This immanent presence is something we can detect in our lives, especially if we have developed our spiritual literacy, our capacity to read God between the lines. At the same time, God is transcendent, absent, wholly other, a mystery completely beyond the grasp of our understanding. This is certainly a common part of our experience as well — those dark moments of doubt, of acutely feeling God's absence.

Where these experiences of the two natures of God merge within our own living, there is our inner life. Deep within, our souls dance between the poles of knowing and unknowing. The spiritual conversation, the journey, the adventures begin and end right there. Each and every one of us partakes. This is Merton's message, as it is the message of our whole Christian mystical tradition.

To paraphrase the ringing conclusion of one of Meister Eckhart's sermons: Your living is a quest for meaning, fulfillment and wholeness. Cultivating your own inner life is a key point of entry. Yearn to know the meaning of your own life. Become aware of what is in you. Cultivate those Godseeds inside. Groan and cry out in the great labor of giving birth to them. Joyfully announce them. Pronounce them every day, for your life is a sacred adventure.

Daybreak Within

When Jesus said, "The reign of God is within you," he was looking right at *us*, not at a rabbi or a bishop or Shirley MacLaine. Most everyone agrees that divine revelation is found in our religious traditions, and especially in Scripture. Because of our modern ecological predicament, however, we are rediscovering the fact that revelation is also surely found in nature, in those lilies out in the field, in the sun's bounteous harvest, in the book of creation itself — and in our own individual lives. Our lives are after all the pages from that book of creation we know most intimately.

"Where can I go from your spirit?" the psalmist sang. "From your presence where can I flee?" This whole question of the divine presence and where it is located is an enormously important one. In the middle years of our century it was commonplace to speak of God's absence or even death. In recent years, however, we have seen a broad move toward acknowledging the indwelling divine presence within nature, within the ten thousand things of creation. Our current ecological crises demand this change in point of view. Some, especially New Age-type thinkers, perhaps push it all too far, divinizing everything or at least making the human ego divine. On the other end of this spectrum many scientists reduce everything to a purely mechanistic grind, refusing to acknowledge any reality besides one molecule knocking dumbly against another.

Our culture today no longer trusts in purely theological explanations for the origin of the cosmos (and of our human life). At the same time it is moving quickly away from a largely mechanistic, closed view of the universe. Most scientists now acknowledge that the natural world in both its widest and narrowest dimensions seems to be an open and creative interplay of dynamically pregnant chaos and of mysterious order — and of profound interrelationship (everything connected with everything else).

It would be surprising if our religious sense and our spiritual questioning were not influenced by this shift. Our religious sensibility has too long viewed our world, at best, as neutral and secular or, at worst, sinful, godless and graceless. It has been taught that God's grace appears only as an intervention in the world's history, as something that disrupts the flow of ordinary, secular life. But another view is coming to the forefront. This view assumes that the universe, from the first instant of its existence, has been saturated with God's grace and presence. From that very first instant of exploding light, God has been seeking, in love, to impart the divine self into things. Far from being a neutral cipher, nature is exactly that reality upon which God's life is bestowed. In the words of Christian theologian Karl Rahner: "Nature is always graciously endowed with God's self."

This leads to a new way of experiencing God in nature, in creation and in us. As a result, the tone of our religious questioning is fast changing. We view the divine as the creative source, the loving heart, the newest deep-down freshness in things, the daybreak within. Annie Dillard writes: "The universe was not made in jest but in solemn incomprehensible earnest. By a power that is unfathomably secret, and holy, and fleet. There is nothing to be done about it, but ignore it, or see." To be religious nowadays we must not only be morally blameless and steadfastly pious, but also we must be wide-eyed, keen and awake. And we need not be shut away in a cloister or remote hermitage; we can be deeply involved in our own living, for each and every one of our lives, no matter how humble or ordinary, is a sacred adventure.

Give Birth to Yourself

On one level, our individual biographies as they are lived out from day to day are answers to a question posed to us at the time of our physical birth. As we live, we give birth to ourselves more and more, and that birth and life are a meaning in and of themselves.

We are, in our own human intricacy and depth and breadth, volumes of revelation and books about God. Our lives, especially our inner lives, reveal the divine mystery busy down there inside things, rummaging around doing what divinity does best: loving and creating and showing off. Often that mystery is found in the very last place we think to look, in the most unlikely places — like in among the straw in a stable, or even in a lowly, surly adolescent. Anyone who's ever lived with a teenager knows this simple fact: There is no power on earth stronger than the human urge to display, to show the world who we are, what we want to become. When I was eighteen, nothing was more important for me than to remind the world that the music of Jimi Hendrix, Neil Young or John Lennon was the equal of Frank Sinatra's or Duke Ellington's. My longish hair, my poster-bedecked bedroom, my bell-bottom jeans and tie-dyed shirts were worn proudly, conspicuously, defiantly. In recent years roles reversed, and I watched my teenage stepson show me and everyone else who he was: with a distinctive haircut etched with razor-hewn zigzags, his bedroom papered with blowups of the Michaels — Jordan and Jackson — of M.C. Hammer, of Malcolm X. The house shook to the heavy percussion and in-your-face dissonant harmonies of hip-hop. But, of course, such has ever been the case. When the walls of the bathhouses in ancient Pompeii covered by Vesuvius' ashes were dug up, they were found covered with graffiti.

We must tell others who we are, no matter what. It's a basic human need, to turn ourselves inside out. Just killing time? No, in the ruckus of our lives we glimpse hints of the holy, signs of the Mystery, and we *must* tell others the story. In the midst of our everyday babble and business we stumble on glory and we must somehow show it off, flaunt its residence within. Grace and divine mystery plant an image in our heart that begs to be expressed and lived out. This image gives rise to yearnings, wild longings, a burning to do the work that fulfills the image. We either yield to this image, or bury it.

Our days are full of chores, appointments, things to do — but also a beckoning wish to decorate our room, tattoo our forearms, confess our fondest wish, update our photo album, pen a good letter, paste up a collage, make an artful decision, fall in love, brag out loud or mount an insurrection against some unjust condition. This force urging us to create, to display, to tell our story, to act creatively, is, no doubt, the passion of divine revelation itself. There seems to be something of the graffiti artist in God. "Divinity is seeking to be revealed everywhere," says Meister Eckhart. "Every creature is doing its best to express God."

Our Inner Life in Context

Is that all there is to it then — just finding our light and then letting it shine? A paradox here is that our biographies don't really belong to us. Our religious quest is done ultimately for the good of the community. In the end we can't help but be members of the global tribe. We must creatively give birth to ourselves for the benefit of the whole Earth. It may well be a key antidote to the addiction and consumerism that take such a toll on the planet's resources, this creative activity of weaving the discordant elements of one's life into harmony and significance, of discovering the fascinating sumptuousness of our own inner life, then connecting our gifts, talents and energies up to good work that needs to be done in our world. "It is no longer possible to believe," writes E.F. Schumacher, "that any political or economic reform, or scientific advance, or technological progress could solve the life-and-death problems of our current society. They lie too deep, in the heart and soul of every one of us. It is there that the main work of reform must be done." We need to explore our inner beings, our heart and soul, search for the causes of our violence, greed or apathy, uprooting them. We must identify our talents and gifts, then reach out with these to a world that desperately needs what we have to give.

As storyteller Garrison Keillor has said, "Life is complicated, and not for the timid." Very often our inner life is all about struggle, wrestling with the oppression of our own inner demons or fighting the injustices we see in the world around us. When we squarely face these inner struggles and outer challenges, we often feel thoroughly overwhelmed. We are unable to adequately nourish our inner life, or we don't know how to bring our lives to these challenges in an effective way.

The Christian spiritual tradition has always offered resources for this part of our spiritual questing, aids such as spiritual reading, meditation, prayer, the art of letting go, the sacraments of reconciliation and healing, all the various spiritual devotions and disciplines. In recent years, for example, the disciplines and joys of journaling have been rediscovered and reinvented. Old prayer forms like the *lectio divina*, a way to bring one's life to Scripture for insight and guidance, have been revived. Active imagination, an ancient prayer form, has been dusted off and refurbished. Spiritual direction, once available only to those in religious life, is becoming more and more accessible to everyone who needs it.

We likely spend our whole lives searching for the balance between interior and exterior, between contemplation and action, working amidst the inner contradictions that make up the human soul. Prayer and meditation are key prerequisites for movement forward in the inner life, for the avoidance of floundering and confusion. "Without this one-hour-a-day-for-God," wrote Henri Nouwen, "my life loses its coherency and I start experiencing my days as a series of random incidents and accidents." Spiritual guides over the centuries have all recommended regular prayer times as the single most important practice in spiritual living. Here is where we can bring the current events and challenges in our days, the overarching themes of our lives, the challenges and dilemmas of our times together with the peace and illumination of God's intimate spirit within us.

The local church is also a place to which we bring our inner lives, our personal stories, our spiritual searching. Gathered together with others we can celebrate and find our lives validated in our spiritual community and its traditions. John Shea wonderfully defines church as the place where we come together, tell the stories, break the bread. Often the story we tell in church is the Scripture story. We proclaim this story in all its richness and complexity. As we do so, as we hear it, we let its meanings sink into our souls. If we have gone astray down some futile path in our spiritual searching, the church community is also there to gently but firmly bring us back to a road that leads somewhere. If we have lost sight of our goals or jumbled our priorities, church can serve as reminder, inspiration, beacon and guide. It is the presence of a community of seekers and searchers, together with an ancient spiritual tradition, that makes our churches such key assets in the inner life and the spiritual questing. Also in our churches we can hook up with community-healing tasks that need to be done.

Divinity can dwell within us, and we certainly abide within divinity. Awakening from its slumber is that insight and knowledge — ever ancient, ever new — that we humans, each and every one of us, are part of the revelatory history of the universe. Each and every one of us is directly engaged in the great work of the world which gave us birth. Salvation lies not in deliverance from this world but in ongoing good work within it, in bringing the Mystery that dwells within all things to light, to greater fruition. The cosmos has furnished us with hands and with prayer, with brains and with a capacity for awe and love — it is part of the Godseed within us to do this good work.

Day breaks within you. You are going where no one has gone before. There is an inner truth in you, an image in your heart, that is absolutely unique to you, and it cries out to be expressed, to be lived out. Your life is a sacred adventure.

Is there no rest? No, only journeying to be yourself.
And even as the Birthmark vanishes, in seashell ear
Now fading to a sigh, God's last words send you in the world:
"Not mother, father, grandfather are you.
Be not another. Be the self I signed you in your blood.
I swarm your flesh with you. Seek that.
And, finding, be what no one else can be....

I circumnavigate each cell in you.
Your merest molecule is right and true.
Look there for destinies indelible and fine
And rare.
Ten thousand futures share your blood each instant;
Each drop of blood a cloned electric twin of you.
In merest wound on hand read replicas of what I planned and knew
Before your birth, then hid it in your heart.
No part of you that does not snug and hold and hide
The self that you will be if faith abide.
What you do is thee. For that I gave you birth.
Be that. So be the only you that's truly you on Earth.

— Ray Bradbury

Sculpting Mashed Potatoes

As a kid, when adults asked me what I wanted to be when I grew up, I'd answer right back, "A forest ranger! Or a priest!" Up on a shelf in my boyhood closet, corroborating this confusion, were my implements for playing mass (a metal cup used to press hosts out of stale Wonderbread, the homemade vestments) right next to my hiking boots and nature field guides. In my photo album lurks a fuzzy snapshot of me as pre-teenager, enrolled in the local diocesan seminary but dressed for a weekend in the backwoods. Torn then between being a wilderness hermit and writer or a man concerned with public liturgy, counsel and prayer, to this day I haven't really resolved this conflict.

When Charles Lindbergh was a boy, he was plagued by nightmares of falling from high places, and he even tried to meet the fear by jumping out of trees. Did his deep innards know even then that he was destined to solo the Atlantic? Surrealist painter Salvador Dali was a kid once, believe it or not, and it is reported by playmates that one day he bit into a rotting bat, a surrealistic act if ever there was one. Schoolmates of Robert Baden-Powell, the British founder of the Boy Scouts, witnessed that he was overeager, always ready to be useful to his teachers, to keep his friends amused, to help older people. Interesting, huh?

Each human life must, after all, be an organic thing, like an oak tree. That tree begins with a blueprint built into genetic material in the lowly acorn, and, obedient to that vision, the tree goes dutifully from sprout to sapling to full-fledged oak. Perhaps we humans are the same, developing according to a blueprint that is beyond the pure biological and latent in the embryo and seed of us. Psychologist James Hillman suggests that, instead of studying developmental psychology, we should study *essential* psychology. The question for psychology, when presented with the bafflingly complex behavior of us human adults, is not, "How did I get this way?" Rather, it may be, "What does my acorn or, better, my birthmark — that image in the seed — want of me?" The key to our life perhaps lies not so much in the events of our living, what happens to us, as in that fateful seed-image, that original vision of what we are meant to be, from the moment of our conception or before.

I wonder if the whole identity-in-diversity question doesn't go much further than just the four or nine types we see in the Myers-Briggs or Enneagram models . . . down to that unique individual image that resides in all of us five billion types on the planet. It is as if the moment we are born, the universe asks a question, and our lived-out life is the answer. "Events grow," wrote Ralph Waldo Emerson, "on the same stem as persons." Our individual biographies may be more impor-tant than we think.

This century's science has altered the way we look at everything. The old Newtonian clockwork cosmos has given way. Now the universe is described by relativity theories and by quantum mechanics, and it's more like that curious storybook wonderland into which Alice plum-meted — a huge swarming of ghostly particles in energetic communion with one another, bubbling up and bursting out of nothing to expand, along with time itself, into immensity, and one in which the whole is physically implied in each of the individual parts. The ultimate aim of this universe, says cosmologist Brian Swimme, seems to rest in each particular being. "The same creative power that created the galaxies and stars is heavily invested in us. We are each given a quantum of energy at birth and we have this task to accomplish: to identify who we are." This is our primary responsibility. Where is the cosmic adventure taking place? In each and every one of us. We must give birth to ourselves.

Steven Speilberg's popular movie *Close Encounters of a Third Kind* provides a perfect image for this dynamic, a nutshell sketch of the mystical quest. In the film, a number of people in a small Indiana berg find themselves sharing a compelling inner sense that they must get to a particular location soon. Deep down, they feel themselves "invited" to this place, and each one finds himself or herself trying to draw, sculpt or paint his inner image. One character uses mashed potatoes. Everyone else thinks they're nuts. But, regardless of consequence, each one does what needs to be done to get to that location — a mountaintop in Wyoming. Haven't we all felt this way at times: invited? What is this inner image in you like? What did you most want to be when you grew up?

A twist here is that our biographies aren't really ours. Our religious quest is done for the good of the community. We must creatively give birth to ourselves for the benefit of others, for the sake of the whole Earth. It is a creative process of weaving all the elements of our lives into harmony and meaning, of discovering the fascinating sumptuousness of our inner life, the birthmark blossoming within and without. All the rest is just smoke and mirrors in the end.

In *Close Encounters*, the end of each one's quest was a communally shared, awe-filled contact with benevolent wisdom, power and delight. Maybe each of us — in our own unique way, of course — is bound for a mountaintop, for similar close encounters.

They Shout. I Follow

My oldest friend, Paige, was always fascinated by the sea, its lure and lore. When he was a kid, model ships cluttered his room, posters of sails and nautical charts papered the walls. He would rhapsodize about his passionate love and his dreams until we his friends got the picture.

The picture looked like this: Paige on the slippery deck of a sturdy sailboat on an agitated sea under a dark, threatening sky. He is reefing the sails and securing thick, sodden lines on the deck, preparing for a storm. One arm flung across the sun-cracked paint on the mast, his hands wrapped in the rigging, he surveys the heaving and leaping surface of the sea ahead with steady, glittering eyes.

Adult responsibilities eroded his consuming passion to a hobby, but Paige took his dreams seriously. A persistent lament for his unrealized vision of living life to the fullest once broke shackles. He ached for the opportunity now and then for the blood to sing in his veins, for his courage and resources to be tested out in the cloud-shrouded Pacific dark. So one day he ordered plans by mail, rented space at the marina in Oakland where he lived, bought plywood, nails and glue. In his spare time he built a boat — a twenty-six foot cruising trimaran, to be exact. He named her *Heart of Gold* after a Neil Young song. On weekends, he'd sail his elegant craft on San Francisco Bay, around Alcatraz out to Angel Island and back. That's not the end of the story. Today Paige earns his living building and repairing sailing craft. I believe he's a very fortunate man.

"By the time many people are fourteen or fifteen," mused science-fiction writer Ray Bradbury, "they have been divested of their loves, their ancient and intuitive tastes, one by one, until they reach maturity, and there is no fun left, no zest, no gusto, no flavor." Reflecting on his own long career as a writer, Bradbury claimed zest, gusto and flavor were alive and kicking in his life because he was above all a hostage — hostage to his passions and loves. "You see," he explained, "my stories have led me through my life. They shout. I follow. They run up and bite me on the leg.... Then, when I finish, the idea lets go and runs off." The end result was a life lived as a fascinating adventure.

"Follow your bliss," advised Joseph Campbell in his famous interviews with Bill Moyers, stressing the importance to the spiritual life of cultivating our unique interests and passions. In what do you most delight? Where is your heart of hearts? To what do your body and soul wholeheartedly want to go? What makes you enthusiastic? Campbell's bliss was studying world mythology. Sail and the sea were Paige's deepest loves. Yours might be growing orchids, quilt-making, home schooling your kids, union organizing, playing in a bluegrass band, ballroom dancing, finding and listening to vintage jazz recordings, writing haiku poetry, constructing your own log house, teaching fourth grade, grassroots political activism, refurbishing old Harleys, your current ministry (lucky you!), contemplative walking, the Grateful Dead, starting recycling in your neighborhood or office, fine liturgy or photography or cooking vegetarian, achieving justice in Central America or in your own workplace, gardening, cooking and eating fiery Cajun dishes — you name it! You know what they are!

Our enthusiasms contribute to our unique personalities. When we find and poke at them, it's like probing a fat throbbing nerve made of glee and joy. Christianity is a religion of incarnation and sacrament, recognizing that the Creator and Sustainer acts in every human life. Yes, as Jesus said, "The reign of God is within you" (Luke 17: 21). Could it be that divine mystery and grace dwell especially at the level of our unique, one-of-a-kind individuality? This makes such sense that the idea is even built into our language. Where do we find ourselves most unique? In those places within us that give birth to *enthusiasm*. The word literally means "God within us." Divine life is found in our true delights, and in the zestful, flavorsome adventure that comes when we follow our passions. Frequent encounters with deep gladness are a sign you are living fully, fruitfully and creatively. Cultivating a spirituality involves locating and exploring those places in the soul that ring like jubilant wind chimes in harmony with the breezes and whispers of the divine.

Instances of cults and fundamentalism gone awry, like the conflagration in Waco, Texas, point up the tragedies that follow when the inner life is not honored and we're thus cut off from the guidance of our own souls, from our best enthusiasm, from Mystery hard at work deep within us. We become prey to manipulation and often surrender to the pat answers of bad religion. Campbell suggests that a reliable spiritual guide is that which brings a flush to our cheeks and a spring to our step; he identified this bliss-following as "the soul's high adventure." "Drunk with life," Bradbury describes it, "and not knowing where off to next. But you're on your way before dawn!"

Frederick Buechner wrote: "Neither the hair shirt nor the soft berth will do. The place God calls you to is that place where your deep gladness and the world's deep hunger meet." Bliss-following is not self-indulgence; it's finding where your best energies can heal and build up your relationships, workplace, neighborhood, country, planet. Our bliss, our deep gladness, has its roots both in heaven and deep within the human community.

As you listen carefully to the deepest, truest whispers of bliss within, they soon echo off the walls of your soul and resound. Follow these shouts and live enthusiastically!

Boxes and Daydreams

Browsing the classifieds recently, I noticed a real estate ad listing one home's major selling points as: one-half mile from schools, two from the nearest mall. In the same paper was a short piece about folks vacationing at the huge Mall of America in Minnesota. It reminded me of what rock star Bruce Springsteen once said in an interview, that all those consumer items, imported electronic toys and designer garments, the baubles and trinkets we buy at the mall, are the booby prizes offered in exchange for giving up any chance at meaningful work, healthy self-respect and a real say in the life of our communities or nation. We get to roam the shopping malls while wealthy corporations get to run the world.

I just finished a novel whose main character was a quadriplegic, confined to a wheelchair, unable to care for himself. Yet he claimed he was supremely happy because, as a result of his disability, he both *knew* he was dependent upon others, on community, while at the same time he possessed a rich inner life. Are not these the two treasures we surrender at the door of the mall — community and inner life? Both are mainstay human nourishments. To be fully well we need places where everybody knows our name, and we need a lively world inside of us. Our society is plagued by an epidemic of anemic self-worth. Who are we beyond our work roles, our professions? Only participation in community together with deep connection through an inner life can give us these answers. Only the energetic crafting of a soul connected with others can enlarge our identity and give it meaning by linking it with all of creation.

Psychologist Dan Montgomery describes a method he uses with clients that often opens up for them the adventure of creatively exploring inner life. First, one selects a box of any size or shape to symbolize one's whole person — a shoe box, a hat box, whatever. Then Montgomery has his client collect photos, images cut from magazines, drawings, words, poems or objects that represent different aspects of that person's life. The box's outside represents the outer shell one shows to the world. Inside the box, Montgomery encourages the client to select and place images that represent the inner self — one's dreams, feelings, secrets, desires and most intimate experiences, yearnings and creative urges. Clients construct interesting, colorful collages, particularly inside the box. Montgomery describes a male client who brought him a box richly decorated on the outside but bare on the inside. Decoration of the box became a real catalyst for that man opening to growth in his life as he searched for colorful, expressive images for the inside. As intimacy with his inner world grew, the box began to fill with balloons and fantastic pictures.

A way I have found to quickly get in touch with my own inner life is to make a list of the people in the world (living or deceased) I currently most admire and wish to emulate in my own living. Whose lives and examples stir my blood? Carl Jung wrote that the qualities we most admire in others, especially in figures who are a bit larger than life, our heroines and heroes, catch our imagination in a vivid way because they mirror qualities that exist within our own soul — those traits and virtues we most value and want to bring to life creatively inside us and in our living.

Try making such a list; it will reveal a lot to you. Some names from my most recent list: artist Grandma Moses; E. F. Schumacher, alternative economist and author of *Small Is Beautiful: Economics As If People Mattered*; Edward Abbey, author of *The Monkey-Wrench Gang*; children's book illustrator Maurice Sendak; singers Van Morrison, Townes Van Zandt and Suzanne Vega, journalist-author Studs Turkel, artist Henri Matisse; all the people who volunteer at school crossings each day; musicians Miles Davis and Professor Longhair; playwright and president of the Czech Republic, Vaclav Havel; political activist and editor of *Sojourners*, Jim Wallis; Catholic Worker founder Dorothy Day; authors May Sarton and Starhawk; documentary filmmaker Michael Moore, who made *Roger & Me*; Miriam McGillis, founder of Genesis Farm; geologian Father Thomas Berry . . . the list goes on and on. My roster of the admired tells me a lot about my own inner landscape — qualities most important to me (such as imagination, humor, outreach to others, commitment to healing the planet) — how I would like to be, what I aspire to. Make a list of your own!

Our inner experiences, it seems, are more trustworthy than we can imagine. Our friendships, relationships, struggles at home and at work, our best dreams, enthusiasms, our inner conversations and adventures supply much that we need to flourish, grow and become better humans. A person with a strong inner life is often dismissed in our culture as a dreamer or an "airhead." Yet consider that the two greatest advances in modern science, relativity and quantum theory, were both arrived at intuitively, imaginatively — even in daydreams. It is reported that Neils Bohr, the father of quantum physics, came to his conception of electron behavior after daydreaming one night about skating rinks. Albert Einstein stumbled on key components of relativity daydreaming about riding sunbeams.

What a pair of space cadets! Yet see what lots of good stuff inside the box can do!

That's Nunsense

The play *Nunsense* hit the local dinner theater recently, poking raucous fun at the experience of growing up Catholic. Dressed in cassocks, wimples and big rosaries, young thespians lampooned the indulgences, pious devotions and simple theology of our youth. My mother's friends dragged her to see it. She phoned the next day to tell me how much she hated it . . . which got me thinking.

Confessing that I have made jests myself at the expense of that pre-Vatican II world, here I wish to praise my Catholic upbringing and wholeheartedly thank those women religious who had a part. Sister Mary Bernadette and her ilk may have (with help from *The Baltimore Catechism* and hyperactive theological dualism) seeded sexual hangups or that aberrant sense of guilt that has taken so many counseling sessions to overcome. But her kind also provided rich nourishment for a way of living, a spirituality that I have come to see as the pearl of greatest price. "The religious attitude," says artist Frederick Franck, "is rooted in wonder at the mystery of sheer Being, in the axiomatic certainty that there is a meaning in our being here, in radical openness to that meaning." Attitude, as they say, is everything.

My own religious sense did not arise the first time I heard tell of the Immaculate Conception or the Real Presence. It awakened in kindergarten when my favorite cat perished under speeding wheels. Why did Pawpaw die? Where is she now? Nestled in the humble manger of my astonishment, it incubated as I looked around me and asked: Where was I before I was born? Why does the starry night sky thrill me so? Why does the mystery of summer cicadas and sweet-sad birdsong make me sometimes ache with nameless longings? Why must Alva Bunting up the street, such a good woman, suffer so cruelly from polio and arthritis? Why does a mere glimpse of her daughter, Rita, with her raven hair and heavy-lidded brown eyes, set my scalp tingling and my heart pounding like a jackhammer?

Our Lady of Lourdes School offered a beginning at answering

these questions — and not just by providing dogmas to memorize and Sunday homilies to drowse by. My teachers bricked-in the foundations for a spirituality, the ground floor of an ongoing encounter with a tradition of wisdom, complete with techniques for prayer and strategies for inner work and conversion. Around experiences and questions like mine, they mounted a scaffolding of faith in things unseen but hoped for. The sisters provided a container — not a perfect one, but workable — into which I could pour my striving to make sense of my life and the world around me.

My Catholic education stressed church authority and offered pious devotions but also, at its best, greenhoused a seedling sense of the world's sacredness into growth. The Sisters of Saint Joseph challenged us with concepts like social justice and democracy, with good story and poetry. They fed our sense of wonder. They pushed wider the circumference of our world. They dragged us (sometimes by the ear) to hear *Peter and the Wolf* or *The Magic Flute*. On recollection days we were required to sit tight and quietly sift our short lives through the sieve of thoughtful contemplation.

Best of all, this education honored the interior life. The sisters, in many various and vibrant ways, taught us that things had an inside as well as an outside, that we each had souls as full of pep as our bodies, that the best and truest adventures are inner ones. They made us less transparent to ourselves and taught us that all manner of fears could be tamed, limitations overcome, boogeymen sent packing through our own inner donkeywork.

In sixth grade Sister Agatha Irene (ahead of her time ecumenism-wise) told us the story of Anne Frank and her family hiding away in an Amsterdam attic from the cruelest organized and jackbooted hatred. Her story froze my blood even more than the fallout shelter signs hanging on the bricks outside. How would *my* faith and *my* integrity hold up, I wondered, in such a terrible proving ground? Where in my own developing inner architecture could the frail egg of courage find a warm place to hatch? Nazis weren't persecuting anyone in 1956, but Jimmy Dozier was doggedly on my tail, providing a crucible that tested my self-worth and sense of honor. The only sure path to that bully's defeat lay in the patient and difficult cultivation of my own virtues. A worthwhile lesson for a child to learn.

For us boys, these women even offered models of males who had deep feelings, tenderness, creativity brooding inside them, someone besides John Wayne and Clint Eastwood to emulate — men like Thomas Merton, Doctor Tom Dooley or Van Cliburn. The sisters provoked growth in the inner life sometimes just by being who they were, by means of their own limitations. Nights after homework was done I would glue my ear to WHB radio until lights out. Somehow I sensed that this new music from the likes of Elvis Presley, Smokey Robinson, Buddy Holly and Chuck Berry would prove more potent than all the Cold War armies put together, that in some unheard-of way it would change the world. Sister Pancratia wasn't having any of it, but I knew she was wrong here — and learned better how to assay, validate and honor my own best intuitions and experiences.

Authentic spirituality is primarily intimately related to our firsthand experience of life. It matures in prayer, reading Scripture, in radical openness to what happens in the workplace, the bedroom, the newspaper, the soup kitchen downtown. That's nunsense!